RY
TEL
LER

First edition

ISBN 978-0-9921071-3-0

Printed in Canada

Design: Mike Berson
Photo of author: Simon Bélanger

BRAM
LEVINSON

Other books by Bram Levinson:

The Examined Life
A Year in the Light

The gratitude I have to this book for insisting on being born despite my best efforts to never go through the book-writing process again is immeasurable. This book forced itself into being during an incredibly tumultuous time in my experience of life, a period in which my soul was transforming despite my resistance to where it was leading me. To quote Bret Easton Ellis, "The book was reliable and I wasn't, not necessarily." Writing this book grounded me and kept me focused when it felt like the world, and my world, were upside down.

This book is also dedicated to Peter Prupas, one of my Keepers, who changed my life in the most important of times and with the seeming effortlessness that was his way.

This one is for you, Peter.

"Whether I shall turn out to be the hero of my own life, or whether that station will be held by anybody else, these pages must show."

– David Copperfield by Charles Dickens

"We discovered that people experienced healing through telling their stories. The process opened wounds that were festering. We cleansed them, poured ointment on them, and knew they would heal. A young man who had been blinded by police action in his township came to tell us the story of that event. When he finished he was asked how he felt now and he said, 'You have given me back my eyes.' "

– Desmond Tutu

"Healing is not born of vanity. It is born of honesty. Honesty is born of pure love. And love is the most divine healer, the sweetest, holiest, and most effective."

– Val Kilmer

This book is written in the spirit of accompaniment. To recount my tales and insights is to reflect back to the reader her, his or their own, and so let this book serve as a trusted friend, resource, support and reference to anyone and everyone who simply needs to feel like someone, somewhere, somehow is there to laugh with, to cry with, to rely on, to walk through this journey of life with.

STORY TELLING

The travertine table. That behemoth of a rectangular stone installation, requiring three burly men to lug into the family home at the behest of my mother and her decorating whims, was the silent presence that greeted and saluted us by the front door throughout our time there. It initially served as the display surface for decorative bowls and sculptures, a backdrop to that which it exposed, but quickly became the canvas on which signs of life rested and were made apparent: the day's mail, a book in mid-read left by one of us en route to the kitchen, a casually strewn winter scarf or pair of gloves left after coming in from the frigidity of the Canadian winter cold. The table was the depository for all things Levinson, including the keys to the cars my parents drove which were a little too temptingly accessible for my fourteen-year-old self.

I have no idea why I decided to teach myself to drive unbeknownst to my parents or my brothers at the tender age of fourteen, but I did. Perhaps it was because I was bored; perhaps it was because I always felt like I was in a race against time and wanted to be older than I was; perhaps it was because I wanted to do what I knew was verboten. Regardless of why, when my parents and brothers were out of the house for long enough and I was left to my own devices, I decided to play with a device that I had no business playing with, my mother's dull, grey, front-wheeled drive Volvo.

I remember the first time I unlocked the car door, petrified that one of my family members would arrive home suddenly and ask me why I was unlocking the car door from the driver's side. I remember how square and clunky the key was and how smoothly it slid into the ignition, the roar of my heartbeat as the engine roared to life. I remember wishing my head had a three-hundred-and-sixty-degree range of motion so I could clock any neighbours who might have been watching from their living room windows as I reversed the car out of the driveway in spurts and starts. I remember the feelings of freedom and accomplishment as I slowly maneuvered the car from reverse to drive and began making my way down the street along which all of my friends and their families lived. I meandered through the neighbourhood, ultimately making my way to a local golf course along backroads and byways before I turned the car around and made my way back. My heart pounded at the fear of being seen as I returned the car to its original parked positioning, the keys to their original placement on the travertine table.

I kept my little jaunts going for well over a year before my last pre-licensed excursion occurred. After zipping around in the Volvo for a half hour on that fated journey, I returned the car back to its original position in the driveway and went upstairs to watch tv in my parents' bedroom which was a floor above the garage. About ten minutes into my viewing, I heard a loud crash from below me and I instinctively went to the bedroom window which overlooked the driveway. What I saw made my blood run cold. The only part of the car (which I thought I had left perfectly parked) which was visible from above was the back half. The car had somehow moved from where I parked it and rolled down the driveway through the garage door.

I ran downstairs, flying over stairs two and three at a time, opened the door to the garage from inside the house and saw that the lower half of the garage door had been busted through by the shark-like hood of the car. My mind went into overdrive. How was I going to explain this? How was I going to get out of the rage that was going to be unleashed on me when my parents discovered that I had been driving their car? I ran to the phone (when it was affixed to the wall and did not follow us around) and immediately called my uncle as I knew that my mother was supposed to be seeing him. I breathlessly asked him if he was with my mother and told him why I was calling. He told me that he had already seen her but that she was already gone. I thanked him and went back upstairs to watch tv while I waited for my parents to return home, knowing they would see the evidence of the crime before I could do any damage control.

They got home together and came into the house with voices raised in worry and confusion. I ran to them and, with as much emotion and mock-innocent sincerity as could be mustered, told them that I had been sitting in their bedroom watching TV when out of nowhere I heard a crash and looked out the window to see that the car had rolled through the garage door. My mother told me that she had looked through the driver's side window and saw that the transmission was in reverse, that it must have given out after being like that for too long, and that she must have left it like that when she last parked the car. She and my father then walked away to deal with the fallout. And I said nothing. I kept that teeny, tiny secret close to me, deciding that if I ever admitted to the transgression, it would be a deathbed confession. On whose deathbed, mine or one of my parents', I had not decided, but deathbed it would be. Instead of waiting for a tragic occasion to come clean, however, I decided to fess up in front of the hundreds of people who came out to the first theatre talk I gave thirty years later, both of my parents in attendance among them. The audience roared with laughter and shock as I told the story. And God bless her, at the end of the show, my mother came up to the microphone placed in front of the seated area for the Q&A portion of the evening to let me (and everyone else) know that "I really just thought it was me".

This book is about storytelling. I never really understood the value of the stories I had about my own life experiences until the 2020 pandemic landed and had me take a good, long look at my past. I had never been someone who looked backwards too much. I was always forward-leaning, onto the next project and adventure. I suppose that I unconsciously believed that to look back was to acknowledge the difficulties I encountered and how they prevented me from achieving the life I thought I wanted. But when the world seemed to stop, when the hum of human industry and activity petered out and I was faced with a seemingly endless amount of time ahead of me in which no projects or adventures seemed possible, I began to peek into the rearview mirror. What I found was that I had stories that I not only wanted to tell, but that were screaming to be told. I also realized that my past never prevented me from achieving the life I wanted for myself, it actually enabled it. It was what I needed to recontextualize in order to transcend.

The need to externalize my stories had little to do with being seen or understood, and more to do with a visceral, albeit uncertain, hunch that in a moment in time when humans were separated and told that togetherness was deadly, my stories could help bring us all together. The hunch was nudging me to unify through the recounting of what I had lived, learned and contextualized, and I would love to say that it was altruistically motivated, solely for the benefit of others, but that would make me a liar. Telling my stories and having them be received was absolutely a tactic for *me* to feel unified as well, to feel part of something, to know that my stories were not living solely within the confines of my mind but rather being shared with others. The expression, "If you want something for yourself, do it for someone else" was absolutely my motivation. The pandemic launched me back into childhood patterns of fear and isolation, but unlike the pandemic, the adult me now had the resources to respond to adversity instead of having it pull me into dark places. Fear had always been a massively successful recruiting tool in my life, onboarding me onto its narratives in the blink of an eye. Thankfully, the spiritual, psychological and emotional work I had done in my adult life had given me the tools to not fall back into that pattern.

Storytelling is the art of recounting details about situations and events, absolutely, but it is way more than that. When you watch a film, read a book, or engage in any narrative that has a beginning, a middle and an end, you are essentially bearing witness to a story unfolding. The reason we have the romantic love affairs we do with Hollywood films and the literary works of art that we collectively celebrate is because at some point in the unfolding of those stories, some aspect of their narratives resonates with us. Some aspect of the story about someone else living something else reminds us of our own experiences, about what we have lived, felt, survived, and recovered from. Fiction, and some non-fiction, in any artistic form, exists to mirror back to us aspects of our own narrative, provoking thought, memories and emotions that remind us that despite the details of the narratives being different, the very experiences of life, survival and being, is common to us all.

We need to see all aspects of who and how we are (and who and how we desperately yearn to be) reflected back to us, even if that reflection makes us uncomfortable. We need to have all aspects of our stories mirrored back to us with different protagonists replacing us in the starring role. When we do, we sometimes become capable of recontextualizing our own dramas and epics, stripping them of emotion and self-inflicted judgement, and tapping into a perception that is closer to reality than to our distorted version of events. Through this lens of clarity is often born objectivity, mercy and understanding for others. We also have a greater tendency to learn important life lessons relating to moral, spiritual and ethical issues through the storytelling traditions of fables, mythology, chants, song, dance, stagecraft, drawings and the written word.

Every single one of us is a storyteller and every single one of us is the sum total of the stories we tell: about ourselves and what has happened to us, about those who have played a role in our stories, about the world and the universe and everything it all encompasses, and how we connect to it all. We are the physical embodiment of the interwoven stories that make up the fabric of the narratives we adhere to throughout life. We are stories unfolding in real time. When that unfolding comes to a halt, the stories remain, and they remain in various iterations. Our stories outlive these bodies in the forms of works of art, photos, books, songs, home movies, and social media, and some of mine will do just that housed in these pages.

The bottom line is that we identify with stories because we have a basic, primal need to find ourselves and the commonality of being reflected back to us. Storytelling is how we unify. It is how we identify. It is how we heal. And, at the end of it all, when the body dies, when the container we inhabit perishes, when life is seemingly gone, what is left? The energy that expresses itself through these bodies we inhabit and, ultimately, the stories.

It is because of this thread of logic that I felt compelled to write this book and title it, *Storyteller*, to tell my stories and recount the wisdom I have amassed before this body I inhabit and manage is no longer and those stories get told by others when referring to the journey of Bram. I was lucky enough to hit rock bottom, to experience my dark night of the soul, when I was very young, and eventually rebounded into a life I love and am grateful for. Along the way, I have amassed some stories. Some crazy, some hysterical, some tragically heart-crushing and some embarrassing, ones that I have been told I must be crazy to share. Regardless, I have some stories worthy of sharing.

I almost called this book, *All About We*, playing off the "All About Me" concept while insinuating that my stories are not just about me, they are about all of us. Because they are. All stories are, ultimately, about all of us, because this experience of navigating life in a human body is what we all share, regardless of how different the narratives may be. By sharing my stories, I have the magnificent opportunity to share the laughs, the burdens, the sadness, the absurdity, the blessings, and the humanity with you all so you can recognize yourself in all of it. We are all orbiting each other in this game of life while rarely coming together in the ways which enable us to thrive, so caught up in our dramas, fears, and hopes, that we often forget just how inextricably interwoven our lives are. In telling my stories, what I am in fact doing is telling all of our stories as a reminder that in a moment in time in which fragmentation and othering have become normalized, there is much that unites us that we would do well to remember.

May this book be a part of the shift towards togetherness and accompaniment in that conversation, and may you, by reading these words, recognize the value of your own stories and journey. May this book wake you up to your role as a storyteller as well. Know that, especially in this particular moment in time, the power you have to heal and unite is a story away, one that you could share through the miracle that is your unique experience and expression. There is only one of you in all of time, and by that knowing, understand that your individual expression and narrative, your story, is not only valuable and miraculous, but also irrefutably worthy of sharing. And may this collection of stories help and accompany you as you navigate your stories, as you seek, reorient, stumble, and thrive on your journey of life.

So, sit back, get comfy, and let me tell you some stories and share some wisdom that will likely make you laugh, cry, cringe, scream and, hopefully, reflect on just how similar our experiences are when the details that typically keep us divided and separated get stripped away. I hope that you find not only commonality in these pages, but that you find yourself realizing that despite these tales coming from me, they are about all of us.

MY SAD CAPTAIN

The slow crawl through Pandemica (the term I have affectionately assigned to the Covid-19 era spanning 2020 onwards) was a laborious moment in time for all of us. A slow crawl out of isolation and, gradually, towards some sense of normalcy, which for me, meant getting back to teaching and coaching in person, face-to-face instead of face-to-screen.

I was seated at the front of the room in an acting studio where I teach with a group of some of the brightest and kindest people I have had the honor of teaching. I was there to introduce mindfulness, meditation and yoga to them. What I have come to learn throughout my career is that while we come together under the labels of whatever work I do in the world, my role is that of connector, to bring people together from all walks of life who normally would not have any reason to cross paths. And so, I was seated at the front of the room, all these faces looking back at me, appropriately masked according to Pandemica regulations, all bodies physically distanced.

The subject matter I was there to share with the students had taken on a different gravitas since March of 2020. I had been speaking to the students about what I consider to be the first spiritual teaching, which is that we are not these bodies that we are conditioned to identify ourselves as being. Bringing this topic up is always the gateway to wonderful, stimulating conversation because the obvious question that this teaching leaves in its wake is that if we are not these bodies that we find ourselves occupying, then what are we? *Who* are we? If we are not the gender of the body, if we are not the face or the waist size or the dress size or the skin tone of the body that we find ourselves in, if we are not the abledness or disabledness of the body, if we are not the visible scars, the beauty marks, the blemishes or the appearance-based personas that we market ourselves as being in our social media profile photos, then what are we?

And so, continuing along the line of this spiritual teaching that we are not the bodies that we find ourselves in, I introduced the students to the core Hindu teaching of one source energy animating all things, all beings, including these bodies that we find ourselves in. I asked the students to consider the possibility that every single one of us is simply an energy that has landed in a body in order to express itself through that body, that voice, that personality, into the world. In full knowledge that I was speaking to a group of actors and actresses, people who had signed up for a career in which expression is a fundamental, foundational building block, I was intentionally weaving in the spiritual significance of expression while tying it back to Hinduism, mindfulness and meditation. My intention in bringing up the topic was to eventually discuss the Hindu understanding of death and how death of the body was undeniable but that the energy which animates the body does not die, but rather moves on to other realms.

I spoke about all of this as an entryway into a guided meditation, the first one of the program. I directed them to focus their attention inwardly, spent some time establishing a steady rhythm to my speech, and then we fell into silence. A few minutes into the silence, as I could see the students falling into their breathing patterns, their bodies relaxing, my phone, which was on the floor next to me, lit up with a text notification from an old friend I had not spoken to in decades. "I am sad to share the news that our friend..." popped up on my screen, informing me that a good friend of mine had passed away suddenly that very morning.

It took two or three seconds to understand what I was reading. And as the news of my dear friend's passing became real to me, I immediately recognized the irony of receiving the news at that very moment. I recognized that this turn of events was meant to be a teaching moment for the students seated in front of me, and for me, the teacher who was always learning the importance of grace and service, especially in the middle of a class.

I quickly focused my attention back to the students and kept the meditation going for another twenty minutes. Once it was wrapped up, I filled them in on the news I had received. I told them that what they were seeing in front of them was what grief could look like when a dash of wisdom and higher-Self perspective was thrown into the mix. In the place of the wailing, sombre, heavy energy associated to the Mediterranean-style grieving process which I had previously been so familiar with, was a joyful, loving, calm, understanding presence. I conveyed to them how as a child I equated death with loss and how much I suffered. I also conveyed to them that through the Hindu teachings, I had internalized and recognized death as being something else. We talked about it, as a group, that morning. We discussed life, death, identity, time, and the responsibility every one of us has to allow our authentic identities to be expressed through the voices and bodies we inhabit for such a relatively short amount of time. And it was through that unfolding of events that we bonded as a group.

This experience of peacefully allowing for death and loss to be included without stigma or drama was a marker of spiritual growth and wisdom for me, and part of a healing process that spoke to my first experience with death and loss which occurred a few days after August 19, 1984. I remember the approximate date so clearly because it was right after my younger brother's seventh birthday, a day that had previously been reserved for celebration and joy.

My younger brother's birthday went as expected, with the usual party with family members and friends. A few days later, as I was getting into bed for the night, our doorbell rang in the early evening.

I remember my mother answering the door and speaking to a girl from down the road who was seven or eight years older than me. They spoke for a few minutes, too far from my room for me to be able to discern what was being said, but close enough for me to identify my babysitter's name being mentioned. My brothers and I had two babysitters who would stay with us regularly on the nights when my parents went out, sisters who lived around the corner from our house. They were only a year or two apart, but as different as night and day. Susie was seventeen, bubbly and boisterous, her sister Cathy more grounded and serious. They were both wonderful people, and we always had a good time with each of them when they came to take care of us. They were two of the major players in my young life, and hearing Susie's name mentioned by the girl at the door immediately raised my curiosity.

The conversation between them ended, my mother closed the door and came to my room where I was already in bed, sitting up expectantly. She told me that there had been a car accident a few days earlier on my brother's birthday, and Susie had died as a result of her injuries. She had been on her way back from the summer camp she had been working at, and the car she had been a passenger in had crashed. Susie was dead.

Even now, I find myself amazed at the intensity and weight of the grief I still feel when I think back to that night. It was the first time I had felt that depth of sadness before. I had felt emotions intensely since as far as I could remember, almost as if I had been born old, an old soul who carried with it into a new incarnation the weight of lives past. The grief I was experiencing, however, was being felt for the first time, and it was deep and jagged, grueling, and relentless, hitting me like a ten-ton truck. The shock of processing life without Susie in it was just that, a shock. The realization that life could be that painful hit me with a brutality and a violence that no one could have ever prepared me for. The realization that Susie had been killed in a car accident kept slamming into me over and over again. I just could not come to terms with the news that my seventeen-year-old babysitter, someone whom I loved and who had taken care of me, was dead. I could not make sense of it. It was incomprehensible, unfathomable, and on a primal level, I did not want to make sense of it. I did not want to accept it, because doing so would make it real, and there was no way that Susie could be dead. The weight of it, the tragedy of it, the horror and senselessness and sadness of it were too much for me to bear.

And so, I started crying. And I kept crying. For months. The grief would accompany me as I woke up each morning from that day onward, and it would get into bed with me every night as I prepared to sleep. It sat in my chest like a lead balloon as I started the new school year, the weight of it crushing me as I reluctantly grew to accept that I was changed forever by what had happened. Trauma tears through the sheaths that separate us from the horrors that life can be peppered by, and the tearing was violent and devastating for me. Coming back to school with this as part of my narrative made me feel even more isolated from my classmates, an isolation I had always felt being a gay kid in a swarm of "normal" straight kids. The grief I started that school year off with stayed with me right through the entire year. It was unpredictable, would swoop in with absolutely no warning, hitting me in wave after wave, often in the most inconvenient times and places, and obliterate any progress I thought I had made in "getting over it" when one wave had subsided. Just when I thought the crushing hold the grief had on me was gone for good, bang, it would hit again.

Unbeknownst to me, life was schooling me about grief, teaching me that it was not something that can be controlled or shelved when its impacts proved to be inconvenient or unpleasant. I was being taught that grief was a process unlike any other I had been exposed to at that young age, a process that would keep me ensnared in its trappings until it had run its course. It also taught me that if you're the one still grieving after everyone else seems to have gotten over it, especially as a young child, you end up walking around thinking there is something wrong with you.

Almost a year after Susie died, I remember playing outside our house and feeling the wave of dread and sorrow reappear, and thinking, "I should be over this by now." I was the only person I was aware of who was still visibly dealing with it, and as grief has us all believe at one time or another, I assumed that there must be something wrong with me because I was apparently unable to get over it. And the even starker truth is that I was not only doing my best to work through the way Susie's body had died, but I was also trying to grasp the depth of the sadness that grief had introduced me to. It was as if I could not believe how deeply gutting the sensations of the grief were, and that, in itself, elicited even more sadness. The sadness opened up even deeper wells and reserves of sadness, of melancholy, of a bottomless pit of empty, heavy, hopeless, hollow blackness. That experience as a child defined my life for decades after it occurred, creating a belief that things would not always be ok, that horrible things could and would happen, and that they were unavoidable. After Susie died, I became a darker version of myself, held hostage by having to carry this grief with me throughout a cruel life. I wanted to be rid of it. I did not want it to be part of my experience. I wanted to reject it and make it go away, because the depression that had followed her passing was the worst thing I had ever encountered, and I felt like I just could not take it anymore. But I did. Because I had no choice. And as the months turned into years, the magnitude of what had happened affected me less and less until I could finally think about it without falling apart. Grief finally showed me some mercy and kindness. Which isn't to say that I got over it. The truth is that I have never gotten over it. At this point in my life, I doubt I ever will. And I have grown to not want to. My experience with Susie's death may have sucked all the joy out of my life at that young age, but when seen in retrospect and through the eyes of spiritual understanding, it was a form of initiation onto this path of teaching and healing, the opening of a circle which closed in that actor's studio, seated in front of all those students as I learned in real time that my friend had passed away.

Another circle opened with my introduction to death and grief. As I grew older and more people I cared about me passed away, an odd, surprising pattern that I eventually understood to be mine specifically established itself, a pattern that started that night in my bedroom with my mother telling me what had happened with Susie.

When I eventually fell asleep after crying myself into exhaustion, I found myself in a dream with Susie. We were at the neighbourhood bakery where both Susie and Cathy would take us to buy candy and chocolate bars. The candies were displayed in cardboard boxes on the glass counter in front of the cash register, and I dreamed that I was looking at them, trying to decide what I should choose. Susie was standing on my right, and I looked at her and told her I did not know how I was going to choose from all the ones I wanted. I looked back at the counter to continue the selection process, and then turned my head back again to look at Susie. She was gone. Sitting on the glass countertop directly in front of where she had been standing was a long-stemmed red rose.

I immediately woke up, sat up in bed and thought to myself, "She's ok. She's telling me that she's ok." I had never been a particularly spiritual child. In fact, I probably couldn't have told you what being spiritual entailed, but once I woke up, I knew what had just happened. I knew that she was telling me that despite everything, she was fine, and while it did not assuage my grief over the next year, it did bring me some semblance of solace and it started a pattern of people coming to visit me in dreams after they had passed away to let me know they were alright and well. After the experience with Susie's passing, every single person who I had known in life came to let me know that they were still around. Always in dreams, always in different contexts and iterations. As a child and teenager, I never questioned these visitations, assuming that everyone experienced them as well, because why wouldn't they? Why would this experience be reserved for me? And yet reserved they were, apparently. Visitation by visitation, I was given tiny morsels of the solace that was waiting for me later in life when the Hindu and spiritual teachings transformed my understanding of death and loss and helped me understand exactly what was happening in those visitations. The wisdom I was sharing with the students that morning in 2020 was wisdom that the school of life had begun teaching me back in 1984, but only recognizable as wisdom after years of life experience and exposure to my studies.

I now know that death is a stopping of the body but not of the energy that animated it. I now look forward to experiencing contact with loved ones who have passed on, curious as to how that contact will present itself. When my teacher Joan Ruvinsky experienced bodily death, I grieved knowing I would not be able to go see her in her home the way I had done for over a decade. I also celebrated knowing that she would eventually make her presence known and that I just needed to maintain awareness to be able to recognize it when it happened, and I absolutely did when she showed up in a few dreams. This education in death, and consequently, in life, has been one of the most important lessons in my life. It is because of its relevance to me that I introduced it to the acting students that morning in Pandemica because if we all understood death not as a full stop, not as loss in its entirety, it could and would change so many key aspects of how we identify ourselves and how we experience grief as a part of life.

We are not taught how to process and contextualize grief in healthy, life-and-death-affirming ways. In fact, most of us learn to deny any talk or thought of death, relegating it to the realm of that which must remain unspoken. This avoidance robs us of the opportunities to find meaning and connection in the ultimate stage of life and prevents us from properly processing the intense emotions of grief and fear. To fully understand death as energy moving on to something, somewhere else, allows us to understand that yes, the physicality of the body is lost, of course. But it also allows us to understand that not all has been interrupted and that we can grieve and celebrate simultaneously, and that those who have shed their bodies are still very much with us. I do not believe that the sadness and grief we each have experienced as we "lost" those we loved was ever meant to remain solely sadness and grief. They were meant to be recognized as the captains steering us towards true wisdom and spiritual appreciation for this experience of life, an experience that can only be fully understood and lived when death, life's demonized sibling, is recontextualized.

ALL THE "ME"S

Over the years I have grown to learn that there are many cognitive parts that make up the totality of who and how I am. I can be shy, ambitious, caring, selfish, hyper critical and judgemental, super compassionate and understanding. Each version of me is a part of me, some heavily influenced by my upbringing and the players in it, while others, I believe, were born with their natural functions.

I have always had a part of me that called bullshit on whatever did not resonate with me (something I have inherited from my father), like the severity of my high school's structure when I was an adolescent. And because I was so familiar with my parents' handwriting, because my memories of sitting next to my mother at the kitchen table of the house I grew up in, me reading a book and her working on the latest *Montreal Gazette* crossword puzzle, were so strong, I inherently developed a way to deal with what adolescence had in store for me.

I can still remember the smell of the pulpy mustiness of the freshly printed newspaper, can still hear the ballpoint of the pen my mom was writing with repeatedly touch down on the laminate tabletop through the newsprint, can still see and smell the fibrous smudge of blue ink that imprinted as the pen pressed down with the inception of the loops and squiggles of her florid penmanship as she filled out letters vertically and horizontally. My parents' handwriting is as familiar to me as my own. My mother's flows romantically, with balloon-y, pregnant B's and far-reaching lower-case L's, her upper-case D's ornamented by twists and coils that initiate and return to the point of inception with a mesmerizing ease and fluidity. My father's handwriting is more of a legal or medical scrawl, with letters that kick off a sentence more completely formed, but which gradually slope downwards to melt onto the line they are written on. As I grew taller throughout my childhood, I grew closer to, and then further away from, the surfaces they would write on, whether they would be filling out crosswords or grocery lists, but in that time when my eyeline was flush with the tabletops of whatever desk or table they would be writing on, I memorized their handwriting.

Having the ability to reproduce their signatures played an instrumental role in how I later dealt with surviving the strict and austere private school for boys my parents enrolled me in for high school. My teen years were very much about creating my own reality while keeping up appearances for everyone else, solely to avoid the fallout of my actions, especially at school. Whenever I and/or my younger brother did not want to participate in whatever gem-of-an-activity gym class had in store for us, I would write us notes addressed to the headmaster excusing us from gym class, written and signed, obviously, by "my mother". Remember, I knew my parents' individual handwriting so well that I could effortlessly replicate eithers' to my (and my brother's) advantage. I was more apt to replicate my mother's handwriting as I knew forging my father's was playing with the fire of his potential temper, but I occasionally took that risk as well. I also took the liberty of writing myself notes excusing me from the occasional afternoon's worth of classes and would head to downtown movie theaters to spend that time in the presence of alternate worlds and narratives. I did it for years, until one day I was called into the headmaster's office.

"Sit down," he told me. I did, immediately noticing that morning's note starkly exposed on the desk between us.

"Your mother did not write that, did she?" he asked.

"No." I replied.

"Very well, go back to class," he said, a wry, reluctant grin forcing its way onto his face.

I continued to skip gym class for the next three years. I spent that time in the library, devouring books and experiencing the felt sense wonder of storytelling. At the risk of more conversations with the headmaster, I continued doing things my own way, on my own terms. Flying under the radar for as long as I could with no one ever the wiser for it was my *modus operandi* until I got caught and had to either change the behaviour to appease others or promise to change the behaviour and then circle back under the radar to keep doing my thing. This was my survival mechanism in dealing with childhood and adolescence and not going absolutely batshit crazy in the process.

Combined with that rebellious part of me that refused to play the game according to someone else's rules was a part with a sense of humour that I inherited from my mother, a part which I appreciate and respect more than I can express in words. This part is as well-versed in coming up with the most inappropriate responses in sensitive situations as my mother is, which almost always reduces anyone involved to serious discomfort or to hysterical, tear-streaming laughter (or discomfort-induced hysterical, tear-streaming laughter). I have learned from the best, what can I say? There are many stories I have involving my mother's proclivity to blurt out what should not be said when it should not be said, but one of my favourites took place when we were cross-border shopping in the US.

When I was a kid, my parents would bring us to Plattsburgh, New York for some good, old mall crawling. Living one hour away from Canada/US border had many advantages back then, one of which being the opportunity to drive down, sweet talk the border agents, go shopping for all the American stuff we could get, then smuggle it back into Canada. Most of what was bought was usually clothing for us kids, clothing we would be forced to wear in layers on the journey back home so that if the car got searched by border agents on the way back into Canada, nothing would be found in the trunk with the "legal" purchases. Coming home wearing four layers of shirts, 2 layers of pants, six socks on each foot and a hat or two was par for the course in those days, and going to Plattsburgh for the day was the greatest treat for all of us. It was truly an event.

Decades later, when I was older, exchange rates were different, malls had withered away and cross-border shopping had become a thing of the past, my parents invited me to come with them to the Super Walmart in Plattsburgh. Gone were the record stores, bookshops and clothing outlets, and in their place stood the behemoths which were the big-box retailers. Despite having no interest in Walmart, a part of me which yearned for those golden days of family outings decided to take them up on the invitation. I had no idea what I was getting myself into.

Once we arrived, my parents each took a shopping cart and split up, divide and conquer-style. I stayed with my mother and proceeded to watch her toss whatever processed food she could find that had ten grams of carbohydrates or less into the carriage. The carriage began to fill up, my parents eventually met in an aisle, decided that they had what they wanted, and we made our way to the checkout line. I should now mention that this story takes place a week or two before Easter, as many of the other shoppers in the checkout lines had carriages filled to varying levels with Easter paraphernalia. I should also mention that at this point in her life, my mother had begun to lose her hearing but had not yet procured hearing aids, so she had a tendency to shout what could have been spoken at normal volumes simply because her own levels were slightly askew.

As we were standing in line waiting behind other shoppers and their Easter-laden carriages, my mother started making clucking noises, apparent to all that she was judging some of what she believed were the more questionable purchases people were making around her. The clucking however quickly turned to high-volume speech when she said to me, "Look at that woman's basket! Look at all that chocolate! Can you believe what she's got in her basket?" I quickly responded in a hushed, discreet tone, "Mom, lower your voice, you're shouting and these people have guns. We are not in Canada. Shhhhh!" However good my intentions were, the delivery was apparently lacking (in volume, most likely) because instead of responding in any way that would have indicated that she had heard me, she rolled her eyes and essentially shouted, "Well, they don't call it Fattsburgh for nothing."

I died. I truly believe that a part of me died in that very moment. From embarrassment, from the fear of being taken out, sniper-style right there in the Super Walmart. I muttered some form of response, helped move the carriage closer to the cash and died a small death right there on the US side of the Canada/USA border.

Now, the proud author and wellness professional part of me would like to think that I have more awareness, tact and the ability to read the room when presented with an opportunity to drop a Bonnie-ism, that I would have a better, more aware gauge of how to go about expressing that inappropriate streak that I have inherited, but I occasionally miss the mark, which happened with her not long after we went to Fattsburgh.

My mother has always insisted on having a cleaning person to help with the housekeeping and has always kept a weekly list of chores for them. While visiting my parents at their home ten or fifteen years ago, I stumbled upon a to-do list for the cleaning lady in mid-completion. From my humble perspective, I have always found humour in the notion that my mother lists the chores she could be doing for someone else to do. In all honesty, I think it has less to do with laziness and more to do with my mother's desire to employ someone and feel like she is helping someone else make ends meet and make a living, but for the sake of comedic value, I digress.

Cut to me finding this to-do list on the kitchen counter:

1) Do laundry.
2) Empty dishwasher.
3) Wash linens.

The list was lying on the kitchen counter next to the toaster with a ballpoint pen lying across it, in mid-completion like a retained inhalation. Incapable of being able to resist putting in my two cents' worth, I picked up the pen (giggling) and added:

4) Re-tile kitchen floor.

I replaced the pen exactly as I had found it and walked away, now uncontrollably giggling (albeit under my breath for discretion's sake). I intended to wait until my mother noticed my handiwork, have a good laugh all together, and then put white-out over it and get on with our day. I stayed at my parents' place for the rest of the afternoon, ate dinner with them, and went home afterwards, my little prank having slipped my mind. My mother did not notice my handiwork that afternoon or evening. She did, however, notice it the next morning, and as I soon discovered, she was not amused.

"Mom! Hi! So great to hear from you in the middle of the day. What's up?" I asked, having picked up the phone at work after being paged on the intercom.

"I saw what you did," she replied.

"Huh? What did I do?" I asked in all innocence and sincerity.

"Re-tile kitchen floor?" she asked.

"Ooooooooooooooh shit," I groaned.

"Exactly," she said, "I saw what you did and I *do not* think it is funny."

"Mom, I'm so, so sorry, I thought you would see it while I was there and we would have a laugh and then I would get rid of it, I am so sorry!" I clumsily stammered and stumbled over the torrent of pathetic excuses that were pouring out of my mouth.

My mother hung up on me. I remember standing with the phone up to my ear, the click of the hang-up resonating, the realization dawning on me that my own mother had hung up on me. I was stunned. It was the most aggressive act she had ever done to me, which, on the one hand spoke to how lovely and loving she had always been, but on the other hand, told me she was properly pissed off. I stood there, shocked and unbelievably embarrassed, holding the telephone in my hand, and then…the giggles began erupting. And what started off as disbelieving giggling slowly grew into a hysterical, high-pitched, desperate gasping for air as the tears streamed down my face and my lungs struggled to inhale as much as possible before raspily expelling it all out through my contracting guffaws. Despite, and perhaps because of, my mother's anger, I thought this was not only one of the funniest moments I had ever experienced, but it was one of the most ironic given that streak of inappropriateness and wickedness was inherited from her. I remember thinking, "Boy, can she ever dish it out, but she cannot take it!"

Coming back to the different parts of me, I also have a part that values concealment. I grew used to keeping secrets as a kid, the biggest of all being my sexuality. Much of my adult spiritual and psychological work has been to let this concealment part understand that it no longer needs to conceal, that there is no threat to survival or safety anymore, but this part heavily influenced me when my partner decided we should go skydiving to celebrate his fortieth birthday. I insisted that we keep the plans from my parents, knowing full well that the news would not be well received. Cut to the two of us meeting my parents for dinner one evening. We had barely even sat down before he smartly said to them, "So has Bram told you what we are going to do for my fortieth birthday?" to which my father replied, "No, what are you doing?"

"We're going skydiving!" he said.

"You're doing what?" my mother asked, her face having gone slack with disbelief, the same expression her mother used to have on her face when she heard something she found distasteful.

"We're going skydiving." I said, praying that the ground would swallow me up whole right then and there.

The silence which followed my words was deafening, broken by my mother saying, "Well, you know that your older brother has gone skydiving?"

"Yes, I know." I replied.

"And you know that your older brother's friend had a girlfriend who *died* skydiving while she was in the US?"

"Yes, I know."

"And you know that your older brother's friend had to drive down to the US to retrieve his girlfriend's body and bring it back to Canada?"

"Yes, I know." I replied, my heart racing with fear as to where this was heading.

What happened next was not what I was expecting, far from it. She went from looking at me to looking down to the floor to the side of her, her eyebrows raised, and in a completely different voice said, "Well sir, do you have anything to declare?", assuming the persona of a customs agent at the Canada-US border asking the guy who had to bring his girlfriend's body back if he had any customs declarations to make.

I honestly was not sure if I had heard correctly. For real. I felt like my brain was short-circuiting, my facial expression befuddled. When I understood that my mother was making a shockingly distasteful joke, the relief in understanding that levity had been introduced into the situation and she was not going to lecture me on the potential dangers of skydiving gave way to me laughing so hard that I ended up crying, all the while gasping to get the words, "You are a sick woman" out of my mouth. She is funny as fuck, and she can dish it out in the most unexpected of ways and moments.

If I inherited the sense of humour part from my mother, my seeking, questioning nature and intolerance-towards-the-nonsensical-and-unjust-in-the-world part comes from my father, a lawyer by vocation who has always walked the line of the fair and ethical. I am always looking for answers, for truth and justice, for understanding and for that which helps make sense of the nonsensical, and as a seeker, I have always had lots of questions. Some of them unbelievably existential, others not so much. For instance, why do men have nipples? Why have I never seen an animal laughing his or her ass off at something that he or she found funny? What happened to Luba (a little Canadiana reference for all of you 80's kids)? Are past lives real? Is karma, as defined by Eastern philosophies and belief systems, real, and if so, how does one explain population growth in humans if everyone is just getting recycled into new baby-bodies? Shouldn't those numbers be declining if we all have the potential to be reborn into the form of a platypus or a condor, thereby striking one more human being out of the equation? Or do dwindling animal populations which are becoming extinct account for the human population growth? If my body dies on any given day, sporting the oversized t-shirt and elasticated waistband shorts that I donned that morning, does my ghost come back for all of eternity in that outfit? Is that my ghost outfit? Should we be asking ourselves every morning when we get dressed whether the outfit we put on is the one we want to be wearing if relegated to an eternity of haunting? Did that group of women who were part of the bridal shower I went to teach a yoga class to all those years ago really believe I was the stripper hired to entertain them or was it a joke? And why on earth are scissors packaged in hermetically sealed plastic casings in stores? If I am buying a pair of scissors, it is most likely because I do not have a pair and need one, so how am I realistically expected to open the packaging to get to the scissors themselves? Thoughts and prayers? A butcher's knife to carefully make an incision and then rip open the plastic packaging? Teeth? A flamethrower? And what about digital libraries? If a book comes in digital format and is carried in said format by libraries around the world, why in the sweet name of baby Jesus would anyone need to wait, in some instances for months, to be able to "take out" that book to read. The library is virtual. The book is virtual. Taking it out is virtual. Every person on the planet could get a copy and there would still be more copies available to other planets and solar systems. But noooooooo, we need to license these books and make people wait for someone to return a book he or she never really took out that never really existed as a hard good that never should have been withheld in the first place. I know, I know, libraries pay for the rights to a certain number of (virtual) books and can only "lend" that same number of books. I get it. It does not change the fact that it is ludicrous. It just is. And what about that drain unclogger that comes in liquid form? Has that ever worked for anyone ever? And what about the fuckery surrounding oral hygiene? Why is it that every time I go to the dentist for a checkup, I get some hygienist or dentist giving me contradictory information and instructions about how to brush and floss my teeth? Every single time! Brush away from the gums, brush in a circular motion, brush clockwise, brush counter clockwise. And why have some of the world's greatest actors and actresses forgotten to properly brush their teeth on camera? Why all the furious, violent horizontal back and forthing as they are frothing at the mouth with pretend fluoride mintiness? And then no rinsing with water when they're done? Just spitting out the toothpaste and getting into bed? Why the insanity? And why were my parents not more vigilant about who they left their children with in their absence when they went away on vacation? Faith and trust in pretty much anyone with a pulse overrode any fear or reservations my parents may have had about leaving their sons as they went to go get tits-deep in cocoa butter on the shores of Bermuda. We were left with cleaning ladies in some instances, and there was even one time when my parents found a couple in their forties or fifties who they did not know and *we* certainly did not know, but who moved in for two weeks, him wearing his stained, white undershirt 24/7 while smoking cigarettes one after the other, her walking around the house like a ghost of a woman who never spoke, but reeking of alcohol. Suffice it to say that by the end of the first week of their absence, my parents' three sons had gone to stay with their grandparents in search of safer harbors. To this day I still have no idea who that couple was nor what they ended up doing for the second week of my parents' vacation. Regardless, I have a part that has some big questions and expects answers that satisfy it. And after years of questioning, a realization that dawned on me not too long ago is that there is so much comedic value surrounding the questions that perhaps the answers do not really matter. Perhaps all those questions are perfect in unanswered form as long as I get a good laugh from them, which is what happened when I decided to try to solve the ultimate question, which is why is it so hard to find the right toilet paper?

Cut to me looking at the toilet paper options at the supermarket, having decided that that day would be the day I would finally discover and buy the holy grail of TP that would become my brand forevermore. As I was perusing the options, the elderly woman standing next to me volunteered, "Don't get that one, your fingers go right through it". Needless to say, I did not buy that brand of toilet paper. And by the way, during the beginning of Pandemica, people around the world were brought to a cognitive state in which the market worth of toilet paper grew exponentially within days, and subsequently went on a loo-roll-buying rampage of Mad Max proportions. I remember thinking a few things when I saw this unfolding in our supposed civilized nations:

1) Is stepping over each other in a mad frenzy to buy up allllll the toilet paper actually the most true-to-reality reality-show ever, with the winner not-so-ironically crowned "The Biggest Ass"?
2) Is not having toilet paper to wipe one's rear end with so panic inducing that it would instigate a national shortage?
3) Is having to wipe one's own rear end with one's own hand the end of the world as we know it?

And while we are on the topics of questions and toilet paper, can we for a second ask ourselves who in their right mind thought that an ad campaign for toilet paper with cartoon bears not being able to wipe their asses properly, walking around with little bits of paper and dingleberries hanging from their butts and then blaming it on the brand of toilet paper they were using, was a good idea????? (If you do not know what I am writing about, look it up). Since when do bears even use toilet paper? And if they had to wipe their asses, would logic not lead one to assume that their talons would not only destroy the toilet paper, but their rear-ends themselves? I will leave that there for you to Google as I digress to more mature subjects that also beg contemplation, but let me also mention that I did not, in fact, resolve the toilet paper issue that day, but rather ended up with good fodder for this book after recounting to that elderly woman how stupid I found that ad campaign with the bears and their arses. Instead of making her laugh, she looked at me as if I had actually exposed my own arse right there in Aisle 5 of the supermarket. She walked away from me shaking her head side to side, and I was once again reminded that perhaps I would have been wiser to have kept my mouth shut instead of letting it go wild. But the desire to find the perfect toilet paper gave me a laugh and a story instead of an answer. And perhaps that was the point all along.

When I now observe my ever-questioning nature and my father's example of not suffering fools gladly, it's easy for me to see how a world built on archaic systems of conformity and belief would land jarringly with me. I can now see why I would respond to the world with objection and disobedience, why I would feel compelled to find new ways, ways that would prove more efficient to me and would circumnavigate commonly accepted avenues of inefficiency and archaism. I can see how this square peg would have trouble fitting into the circular molds that circular people have oft-thoughtlessly and effortlessly fit into for decades and centuries before me. But what I can also see now, through the lens of experience and self-knowledge, is that sometimes the questions born from the seeking mind do not need to produce answers, that being in constant pursuit of logic and answers might prove unfruitful, and that the comedic material and stories lying in wait just might be, ultimately, the reward.

Seeing as how all of who and how I am, how I understand myself to be, very simply and humbly makes up a collection of stories, stories that are ephemeral at best and which will last only for as long as the humans who know them, the ultimate question which comes up is does any of this matter? Does it matter if I matter? Does it matter if my stories are remembered? Does it matter if my expression makes a difference? And mulling over those questions activates more questions. Does it matter if we stand in judgement of each other? Does it matter if we have world peace? Does it matter if we remain divided for the rest of time? Does it matter if there is, indeed, an extinction event that will relegate humans to the realm of the dinosaurs? Does it matter if we ever find long-lasting, sustainable safety and comfort? Does it matter if you have 40,000 followers on Instagram or if your latest TikTok has gone viral? And most importantly, has anyone ever found the holy grail of toilet paper? If I am being honest, I don't know. But ultimately, all these questions point to the volatility of life, of not knowing, of the human brain's need to find stability in a world that never ceases to change, of needing to find an answer that we can digest and move forward with, of needing to have something immovable in the midst of the never-ending kineticism of life. And that has been the underlying theme to all my stories, to all the "we"s in me. Riding out the volatility of life seeking some form of reassurance, levity and stability. As the expression says, there are no truths, just stories, and so what I am left with is that that which I was seeking was that which I was living. It turns out that answers were not what I was looking for, the stories that stem from the questions were. The stories ended up being the only truths dependable and immovable enough to be worth sharing, and the anchors that have allowed me to finally find what I was seeking.

THROUGH THE LOOKING GLASS

I have learned through time and experience that we often have the unfortunate habit of focusing on everything that is going wrong, on all the challenges and worries, yet when the majority of us look back on our lives, those challenges do not necessarily stand out more than the good stuff that coexisted simultaneously. When we are experiencing hardship, it tends to overtake and discount the positive, yet when we reflect on the past the positive is often dominant in our memories. We tend to remember what was going well, not solely what was going badly. That golden hue that Hollywood uses in film and television to romanticize the past is used because it reflects what the human brain often does, which is cast a golden filter on past events and situations, and what we are most often left with is the understanding that those days were golden. In the presence of all that we obsessed and lamented over, what floats to the surface of memory is what made those days ideal.

Identifying in the now what will be reflected back on fondly is challenging, to say the least. Through the lens of understanding and experience I can now weed through what I understand to be the changing landscape, the field of awareness in which temporary highs and lows are just that, temporary, and identify some of what will be treasured further down this path when seen in retrospect. To know my Self as an unwavering, unaffected, observing presence able to identify what pops up in the ever-spinning carousel of the changing landscape, whether that be a negative thought in my mind, a pandemic, a beautiful sunny day, a war on the other side of the world, or an uncomfortable conversation that needs to be had, has been a tactic that has helped improve my experience of life.

The blessings that defined my childhood were greatly overshadowed by the crippling insecurity I felt, and that pattern of suffering trailed into adolescence and still occasionally rears its head. Being chronically insecure ruined lots of potentially great moments for me. If I were in the presence of others, I held everything I did or said under the microscope of how it might be perceived, construed, criticized, or judged. I could not just go dancing with friends and lose my inhibitions by letting go and having a good time. I was too attuned to what I believed I lacked, and that attachment to my perceived shortcomings was present when I felt observed, most so when someone wanted to take a photo of me, or one with me in it. I remember some of those posing moments, thinking that my hair (when I had it) wasn't right, that my smile was too much of this or not enough of that, that my body looked too fat or too thin. As far as I was concerned, there was always something wrong with me and my appearance. The discomfort of being in the Bram body made everything about posing for photos almost unbearable, and really imprinted itself on my memory. Yet, despite all that discomfort and suffering, when, in later years, I would come across the photos in which I had posed with all those cyclonic thoughts and "shoulds" and insecurities whirling around in my mind, I would see that younger version of myself in the photograph and think how incredible I looked. I would look at my appearance in the photos and wonder how I could have been so caught up in the conviction that I looked wrong, faulty, not good enough. I was so caught up in what my mind was finding fault with that I was blind to what actually existed, and what existed I now see as golden. Looking back, I not only see that all the negative self-talk and thinking was just one part of the totality of my life back then which also included blessings, but I also see the negative self-talk and thinking as golden themselves. I see those ages, those stages and chapters of my life, through a golden haze that only time and maturity can produce.

I have become more mindful and adept at being able to flag those thoughts which present when I am tuned into that frequency of lack and know them to be a) unhelpful, b) associated to the dysmorphia we all have concerning how we see our selves, physical and otherwise, and c) most likely untrue. Learning that my thoughts are not always my friend has been a huge help for me in dismantling the structures of self-sabotage and self-destruction I had grown so accustomed to. When I look at my past through this lens, the lens of how harmful my thoughts were when I was too young to know any better, I feel such profound compassion for those younger versions of me, a compassion that propels me to work harder and with more intention to expose what I now know to other people.

Delving into my past is interesting, to say the least, because it tends to ignite compassion for those earlier iterations of Bram while bathing my memories in a golden light. Years ago, I discovered that the sister of someone I knew as a child lived in my childhood home with her own family, so I looked her up on social media and found photos of them in the house that was my whole world all those years ago. I looked at the photos and found myself quickly looking away, as if my retinas were being burned by what they were seeing, my body filled with a beautiful, melancholic, expansive sadness. I quickly recognized that a very fundamental part of me had no interest in seeing something, anything, superimposed onto what I equated with my family home from back then. I know that I grew up in wonder years. Even with the challenges and suffering I survived as a child, I irrefutably had all the comforts I needed, and was surrounded by a tight-knit, loving family unit. I had, in all senses of the word, a home.

"Home" for me is the smell of the Bolognese sauce cooking on the stovetop in the leadup to dinner as I watched tv downstairs in the den. It is Deli Boys, the local delicatessen where my family would occasionally eat and where, getting over a stomach bug, I devoured a smoked meat sandwich after a week of eating tea and toast knowing I would not be able to digest it properly. "Home" is the local supermarket, the bakery, the mall. It is *Video Hits, Friday Night Videos, Good Rockin' Tonight*. It is Saturday morning cartoons and the Saturday night NBC prime time lineup. It is guitar and piano lessons, homework with my mom at the kitchen table, and dancing alone in the den as the music I listened to gave me life through the Marantz stereo. It is snow tunnels on our front lawn in winter and the sound of the lawn mower launching the verdant lushness of freshly cut grass into the summer air. It is the blistering hot summer afternoons with fat, pollen-drunk bumblebees hovering and the smell of the lilac tree. It is the crunch of the cucumbers grown alongside the green beans and tomatoes in the back garden, and the feel of pile carpet under bare feet in the living room. It is Mama Lil and Papa Mac, my maternal grandparents. It is Mom and Dad and me and both my brothers, who we were as a family that lived together. It is the clandestine jaunts in the car that I took while teaching myself how to drive. It is the linen closet, whose top shelf was my favourite hiding place for Hide and Seek, and the basement that was cold and dark before the renovations lit it up and provided two more bedrooms and a bathroom. It is cheese bagels and chicken burgers, warm summer evenings at the park across the street, and the twilight beaming behind the drawn blinds as I lay in bed at bedtime waiting for sleep to come on summer nights. It is the smell of my mother's perfume and my father's aftershave. It is The Cure, Madonna, Peter Murphy, Depeche Mode, Midnight Oil, Ozzy Osbourne, the smell of freshly unwrapped vinyl albums and cassette tapes, and alllll the Sundays listening to *American Top 40* on CKGM on my silver portable AM/FM radio. It is that house, the sixth family member. I would rather remember it how it was with us. With all the trials and suffering of growing up Bram there, there is still this part of me that does not want what I know of that house to be replaced with updated versions and different inhabitants. My "home" is the amalgamation of decades which have been woven and stitched together Frankenstein-style into one idyllic narrative, one that makes my heart squeeze when I think of it, one that I will always carry with me. It is precious and sacred and a moment in time. And I'd rather keep that moment frozen in the halls of my memory remembered through that golden haze. I would rather remember "home" as it was back when it was ours exclusively, even if thinking about it almost breaks my heart.

There is a grief associated to not only that home and the times it represented, but to the past, to my past. Of course, there is nostalgia, which the *Cambridge Dictionary* defines as, "a feeling of pleasure and sometimes slight sadness at the same time as you think about things that happened in the past", going on to specify that the word nostalgia is the learned formation from Greek root words, consisting of νόστος (nóstos), meaning "homecoming" and ἄλγος (álgos), meaning "pain" or "ache". And so, when I look back at my childhood home, there is an ache related to coming home, not only back to the brick and mortar of the house we lived in, but back to the cognitive world I lived in back then. The grief I experience when looking back is one that the adult Bram has understood he does not want to grow out of. I now understand that I might look under the nostalgia and discover that which cracks my heart open, but which does not break it. I understand, through the lens of seeing my overall story and all the substories that contribute to it, that what looks like pain, what *was* painful, is, at the end of the day, a story. The pain and struggle is a story, part of the totality, and what I now know as a storyteller is that I can take everything that I initially thought would kill me and reframe it, recontextualize it, and know it to be part of the process of healing. That world's images, when conjured up in my present-day brain, present themselves almost sunlit from an angle, with beams and rays illuminating the imagery diagonally, creating an almost hazy filter of softness over the memories, even the more gruelling ones. A golden filter for golden times which were, of course, not *only* golden, but that filter imposes itself regardless.

Those years *were* golden because I can now see what occurred during them as golden. And speaking of golden, there was an incident that occurred when I was perhaps nine or ten years old that always comes to mind when I think about those years, an incident that almost got me onto The Graham Norton Show in England.

One lazy summer afternoon I was shooting a basketball in the driveway of our home, throwing it against the garage door and catching it, having a good time all by myself. My mother came out of the garage door with a massive garbage bag full of stuff and told me that she was heading out to run some errands and was leaving me with the bag which was filled with toys that my brothers and I had outgrown. She told me that Mrs. Katznelson, a neighbour from down the street, would be by to pick the bag up so she could pass on some of the toys to her grandchildren. My mother closed the garage door, got in her car and told me that she would be right back, but that while she was gone, I would be locked out of the house because she had forgotten to unlock the front door. Knowing she would not be gone for long, I resumed dribbling the ball and getting back to what I had been doing.

A few minutes later, I felt the need to pee. Urgently. It hit me all at once, and I went into problem solving mode. I was locked out of the house, which meant that I had four areas I could relieve myself: the backyard, the passageways on either side of the house that led to the backyard, or where I stood in the driveway. The front lawn was too exposed, and I feared that by going to the backyard, I would potentially miss Mrs. Katznelson if she showed up for the bag of toys. The side passageways were off the table as the neighbouring houses on either side had windows overlooking them. The driveway it would have to be, I decided, a decision that got reinforced when I realized that once I was done, I could get the water hose from the side passageway next to the garage door and rinse off all evidence of the crime.

I walked up to the sidewalk bordering the street and looked both ways to see if anyone (Mrs. Katznelson, in particular) was in eye-sight. Much to my (and my bladder's) relief, the street and sidewalks were empty. I walked back to the garage door, hooked one thumb under the elasticated waistband of my jogging pants, and with my other hand pulled out my business and began peeing on the varnished wood siding of the door. I felt my body slowly relaxing as I peed, and I may have even uttered a sigh of relief. If I did, however, that sigh was interrupted by someone behind me asking, "Bram?"

My entire nervous system short circuited. Someone was behind me watching me pee on the garage door. And instead of thinking methodically about how to proceed, my nine- or ten-year-old autopilot kicked in. And backfired. Massively. The thumb I was holding the elastic waistband of the joggers jerked away, allowing the waistband to snap back to its original position, but this time, unfortunately, something was obstructing its journey back to my waist. The waistband snapped backwards, hitting my business, smacking it into my lower abdomen pointing upwards towards my face. With my back facing whoever had magically appeared in my driveway and interrupted my moment of relief, my nervous system did not get the message to stop peeing. Instead, because I had been spoken to, my instinct was to respond to who ever had spoken to me, even though I was peeing in my own face. And. So. I. Then. Turned. Around.

Mrs. Katznelson obviously had used some of her ninja skills to clandestinely teleport onto my driveway, but those ninja skills could never have predicted was what she was going to be exposed to when she did. She may have come for a garbage bag filled with old children's toys, but what she got was a nine- or ten-year-old boy peeing in his face as he turned around to respond to her. The look on her face when I turned around was, quite simply, horror. I did not respond, fearing that opening my mouth to utter any words at all would result in a mouthful of urine. I just looked at her. She stared at me for what felt like an eternity before turning away to look at the bag. She looked back at me and asked, "Is that for me?" I nodded affirmatively. She grabbed the bag, and she bolted. I stayed standing there until I eventually stopped peeing, the horror from her face having firmly implanted itself into my brain.

I turned around again, walked to the edge of the side passageway of the house, grabbed the water hose and turned the water on full blast. I rinsed myself off before going full tilt on the garage door, ensuring that I was drenched with water so that any wetness could be explained when my mother got back. When she did and asked me why I was drenched, I mumbled something about needing to cool off and then ran inside to rid myself of those clothes and my shame.

That incident was shameful for me and stayed that way for years and years before I could recognize the flipside of that shame as humour. What landed traumatically for me back then with deep, deep shame ended up becoming the story that makes me laugh uncontrollably and reduces everyone who has heard it to date to tears. That shame transformed into something positive, which was a huge teaching moment for me.

My memories from back then are golden, even the ones that elicited deep shame all those years ago. And they are perfect. Everything from my youth is perfect. All of it. Nothing to change, nothing to fix. It was all happening so I could get here and make you feel something as I share my tales and trials. Has the journey been bumpy, full of unforeseen obstacles of all shapes and sizes? Absolutely. Did I really believe I would die in some of those moments? Undeniably. Do I now know what it was all for? Not sure. I do not believe that everything happens for a reason. I do, however, believe that something of worth can be extrapolated from any and every situation. The lessons are everywhere. And what looking back has done for me is teach me that I could transcend that which I believed would end me, find comedy, life and inspiration from it, and find what I was seeking as a geeky, awkward child, which was connection. This is the human experience. This is Joseph Campbell's *Hero's Journey*. I am Frodo. I am Luke Skywalker (in jogging pants, apparently). I am every protagonist in every work of fiction or otherwise who struggles, transcends that struggle and returns to where they began to be of service. This is what humans do and it is why storytelling is so vital to the lived human experience. How better to reflect back to each other the collective narrative of humanity and being than through hope and inspiration?

And so, if all the moments, all the stories, that unfolded as horrific but through the lenses of wisdom and maturity can now be perceived as golden, then this day must be golden. Today must be golden. Logic states that one day I will look back on this day in time, replete with all that I struggle with as I write these words, and see it through the golden haze, feeling that ache for who and how I was back then, for how blessed I was to have the life I had. This moment is what will be remembered as "when things were incredible".

Recognize. Recognize how you will look back on this phase of your life one day with so much poignance, with so much nostalgia, even in, and especially in, the presence of all the stuff that could drag you down and leave you gasping for breath. There is, and will always be, aspects of now that are ideal, aspects which, in retrospect, are so sweet and sunlight-tinged that they will effortlessly and unconsciously get classified into that heart-crushing place in your memory that elicits all the best feelings and emotions. Recognize now. In doing so, you will end up knowing that you took a second to recognize, appreciate and understand the inherently transient, ephemeral nature of being in that distant future moment when now becomes then.

THE KEEPERS

Like most people who grew up in the eighties, the ultimate in excitement for me as a kid consisted of walking down to the corner of the street I lived on, waiting interminably for the bus that came every half hour (a half hour which, in the hell of Montreal winter, felt more like an eternity), riding the bus as it snaked through suburbia to finally arrive at, drumroll, please… the mall. The mall was the hub of it all. It was where dollars were dropped, slices of pizza were eaten, and where, especially in a northern climate whose winter seemed to span seventeen months out of every year, I could escape my home to go spend hours in the warmth amid the hubbub of hairspray and shoulder pads.

The Cavendish Mall was the epicenter of culture for me, a metaphorical Mecca that seemed so attractive yet mysterious to me that I had childhood fantasies of being locked inside it after closing time, forced to spend the night amid the empty record and department stores and their frozen-in-time mannequins. Regardless of who I was friends with throughout my childhood, one thing was constant, and that was where we would hang out. The *Shmall*, as we referred to it, was our home away from home.

A somewhat unfortunate by-product of my childhood was that although I knew I was physically taken care of, with a home to live in, food always at the ready and a loving family, I never felt at ease or safe. I was a closeted gay kid who felt his secret would out and the end of the world would ensue. It is obvious to me in retrospect that I operated from a massive emotional void, a blank space that throughout the years I tried to fill in multiple ways. Books played a huge role. I was an avid reader as a kid, constantly clutching whatever book I was engrossed in, regardless of where I was. Books were my gateways to alternate worlds, and if I went anywhere with my family, even to other people's homes, I brought my book. If we went to visit my grandparents, I brought my book. If we went to synagogue on the Jewish High Holidays (which we did throughout my childhood), I brought my book and propped it up behind the prayer book.

Music was also an escape, as were television and movies. Anything that uplifted my spirits by introducing other emotions aside from the ones that weighed me down were welcome. But not all the ways I dealt with my struggles were as harmless as reading or listening to an album from start to finish. I also began stealing. It started with taking a ten-dollar bill from one of my parents' wallets every now and again. As I started to experience the not-so-healthy thrill of feeling some semblance of control in my life after years of feeling powerless and helpless, I began trying my luck in stores. A candy here, a chocolate bar there. Knowing full well that what I was doing was wrong, the feeling of being able to control something left me feeling embodied, grounded, alive, alert, connected to a world that I had previously felt only disconnection to. Stealing became my lifeline. Imagine being so uncomfortable and so unhappy in your life that something as immoral and deceptive as stealing becomes your saving grace. And it was for me. Until I got caught when I was eleven years old.

Record stores were a staple of the shopping mall throughout my childhood, and record shopping was an experience that was mind-blowingly fun and irreproducible, even when compared to shopping in today's vinyl-revival culture. The recording industry was royalty, with billions of dollars being pumped into promotion, album releases and album design, and any opportunity to go to the record store was guaranteed to reveal a new discovery, a new release, a new moment of being uplifted by the sheer artistry that existed in the industry back then. It was normal for me to go record shopping at the Shmall every week or two, and one weekend I went with my next-door neighbours, two sisters I was close friends with as children.

We got to the mall, eventually got to the record store, and split up as we perused everything on offer. I remember walking up to the wall where all the colourful music pins were housed, affixed to the wall in a massive mosaic-like display. All the main players stared back at me from their square or triangular shapes: Billy Idol, Pat Benatar, Boy George and Culture Club, David Bowie, and there she was, Cyndi Lauper. My current obsession. I wanted the pin the second I saw it, and without flinching, I looked around, saw no one looking my way, took it off the wall and pocketed it. And there it was, that feeling of being back in my body. I felt the adrenaline pumping, the blood coursing through my veins. I felt alive. I felt powerful. I felt like I had tapped into some secret that no one else knew, one that gave me a sense of superiority and worth after years of feeling so insignificant that I could have disappeared without anyone being any the wiser.

I continued rummaging around the store until my two friends and I were done, at which point we walked back out into the common area of the mall. The guy who had been behind the cash in the store followed us, came up to me, and asked me to show him what was in my pocket. I feigned confusion, as if I did not understand the words that were coming out of his mouth. He then told me, in front of my friends, that he knew what I had done and ordered me to follow him back into the store. My friends were stunned, upset, and I left them there, telling them I would be ok, as I followed the employee back into the shop and into a back room where he called the police, and where I stayed sitting until two officers showed up. They escorted me out of the mall to their car, brought me down to the police station, sat me down and had me wait there. I remember the officers at the station yelling out to me with mock threats as I was escorted to a room. I remember calling home and speaking to my older brother, letting him know where I was and what had happened. My parents were out of town at the time, providing some relief knowing that I would not have to have the discussion I knew was in store with them that same day, despite knowing that it was going to be a difficult discussion once they got back home.

The police drove me home with a warning, and when the car pulled up to my family's house, my next-door neighbours' father was waiting for me on the sidewalk. The police car drove off and I was left with Peter, who had been filled in by his two daughters as to what had occurred at the mall once they had gotten back home. When I first saw him there, I was petrified that he was going to unleash his fury on me at having done something so stupid while with his children, but as it turned out, I had little to be afraid of. He asked me how I was doing, if I was alright. When I told him I was ok, he told me that when he had been a kid, he had stolen some candy from a store. I knew then and there that instead of unleashing hellfire on me for involving his daughters in the situation, he was doing his best to normalize what I had done to make me feel better about it. He told me that although it was something he had done himself, he had later learned that it was not alright, that stealing was not ok and that the situation I was coming out of was life's way of teaching me a lesson. He told me that what had just happened did not mean that I was a bad person, and that it was not an indication of being a "bad kid", and I remember that those words instantly helped me feel less ashamed of myself and this despicable behaviour which I had grown accustomed to. Although I was still unbelievably mortified over the situation I had gotten myself and my friends into (I still remember how sad I felt watching them watch me get caught for something so embarrassing and devious, how truly confused and upset they were), Peter's words helped me to exhale a little deeper and to relax after the trauma of the day's events. He squeezed my shoulder and told me everything was going to be ok. I mumbled something resembling "thank you" despite wanting to run away as fast as humanly possible and then went inside to deal with the fallout of my actions with my brothers and the woman who was taking care of us in my parents' absence.

Peter took care of me that day. He waited outside for me to get home, standing on the sidewalk in front of my house, watching the police car pull up to the curb and drop me off, intent on intercepting me so that the whole ordeal I had just gotten myself into could be buffered with kindness and understanding. After putting his two kids through whatever they had to deal with because of my actions, he was waiting out there calmly and compassionately, intent on helping me feel better. Whether or not he expected me to roll up with that police escort, I will never know because Peter passed away not too long ago, before I could get these words into book form. I wanted to present a specially dedicated book to him in person to thank him for what he did for me that day but life did not conspire to make that happen, and so these words mean even more now that I feel like I am writing them directly to, and about, him with every keystroke.

Peter did not have to wait for me outside. He did not have to be kind to me, or to say or do anything that would help me feel better. To be honest, I expected to either be shunned or to be yelled at, but regardless of whatever fallout there could have been that day, Peter showed up for me. He took care of me in a way that I was starving for, devoid of judgement or any inclination to "other" me with punishing judgement or criticism. He welcomed me home, made me feel understood, made me feel not so alien, made me feel like what had transpired that day did not have to be a defining moment on the road to perdition that I believed I was barreling down. Peter did something for me that day that no one else could have done, something no one else *did* do, and the significance of his actions will stay with me until my last breath. The felt sense of loving kindness that Peter instilled in me all those years ago is what I still carry with me today. It is what informs the inclination I now have to stand in non-judgement of those who transgress, regardless of whether it be to me or in the eyes of the masses. Peter gifted me that energy. That energy now lives on.

My parents and my brothers have also been there for me in key moments in life when I needed to be reminded that all was not lost. I always considered myself to be the black sheep of the family because it seemed like every step of my development throughout childhood and adolescence was out of the norm. Despite having front row seats to my struggles and the choices they may have found questionable, they never stopped supporting me. Whether it was the unfortunate exit strategy I took from the summer job my father got for me (a tale recounted in my first book, *The Examined Life*), friends I had over who my parents did not like or trust, sneaking out of the house at night to go hang out with friends (only to sneak back in later in the wee hours of the morning), or the times I was so lost just trying to figure out what the hell I was alive for, my family always let me know that they always had my back, no matter what.

My maternal grandmother was the same. I spent a lot of time with my mother's parents, and Lillian Berlin, my Mama Lil, was one of the most compassionate people I knew. She loved me big, even racing towards me first thing in the morning when I slept over at her house, her face slick and tacky with moisturizer, ready to attack me with kisses. When I went through an extended moment in my late teens in which I was not working or in school, she was the one who first spoke to me about emotional intelligence. She told me that even if school was not a good fit for me, there were different types of intelligence, and book smarts were not the only smarts that mattered. She told me that value was beginning to be placed on emotional intelligence, which she then defined for me as being one's ability to wisely feel, respond to, and navigate one's emotions. She told me that I had been born with an emotional intelligence that could not be taught to someone who did not inherently have it, and in that one conversation, she conveyed to me that I had a worth and value that perhaps had not been rewarded yet, but that was inherently mine. Much like Peter had done, she did something that she did not have to do in the spirit of generosity, in the spirit of planting a seed of confidence within the wasteland of fear and hopelessness that was my emotional state of being. And much like what Peter had said to me, her words have stayed with me to this day and have served as the foundation from which I have learned to not only be hopeful, but to *be* hope, to be an example of what hope looks like in the world.

The Keepers, as I like to refer to all the people who have ever helped me jump beyond a grim future that I believed was my destiny, taught me that there was more than just the bleak and dismal awaiting me on my journey of life. Perhaps without knowing how meaningful their efforts would prove to be, they taught me that in the presence of the despair I felt co-existed another avenue. They taught me that happiness and fulfillment were possible. They taught me that I wasn't the massive fuck-up I believed I was, that what I focused on mattered, and that staying the course of hope and authenticity would be my life's work. They taught me that the world could potentially open up with warmth, compassion, and understanding for the introverted gay bookworm who felt alone and afraid his entire childhood. Because of them, I later learned that my wounds were not suffered in vain, that my wounds could become my purpose, that all the struggle and confusion could and would serve me well so that I could be of service to those experiencing suffering in their own experience of life. I learned to find value in my uniqueness and honour it as an example to others who needed to know that they were not destined for failure or despair. The Keepers taught me that I could trust and believe in myself, and in hindsight I can see that through them I learned that perhaps suffering is a sign of progress, a sign that growing pains lead to something else and to stay the course and look for the big lessons. The Keepers taught me that I was ok.

If life can be likened to a video game, and one cannot unlock access to future levels and worlds without first facing the most monstrous of demons, then my game-of-life experience had me levelling up at an early age. The Keepers helped me to understand all of this. The Keepers saved me. In doing so, they taught me that it was possible to not only reset the course of one's life, but to then pay the kindness and love forward and be a Keeper for others. They taught me that my stories, my individuality, my life had value. Without them, I would not have recognized that value, and if I had not been inspired to show up as myself fully, these words would not exist. This book would not exist. None of what I have put out into the world would exist. This expression would have stayed silent and meek. It would all be missing from the world. And so, when I am asked what I do in life, what my "career" is, I no longer tell people that I teach or that I write, that I lecture or that I bring people around the world. I simply tell them that I accompany others and do my best to be a Keeper for anyone who is open to accompaniment and who is ready to see their narrative and the future of that narrative through differently tinted lenses.

I am a Keeper. And in choosing this life of a Keeper, because do not kid yourself, every single aspect of how we show up in the world and in our lives is a choice, I intentionally carry with me the kindness, the generosity of spirit, the time, energy, and the spirit of accompaniment that those Keepers who came before me offered me without any expectation of anything in return. Thank goodness for The Keepers. May we all strive to be that for others along the individual paths that we trek through life. And may we all take a moment of reflection to consider our Keepers and offer up our gratitude to them.

THE LEGACY TEACHINGS

Over a decade ago, I was given a copy of a memoir written by my maternal great-grandmother, photocopied type-written pages bound simply in a pale blue duo-tang folder. I tucked it away on a bookshelf after quickly scanning through it and would later pick it back up occasionally to read excerpts, but truth be told, I would read a few paragraphs and then close it, put it back on the shelf and leave it there until it next crossed my mind.

I came across it again a few years ago and decided to finally and properly read it in the same way I would a book. I sat down with these pages that contained a good chunk of my maternal family's history written in my great-grandmother's own words, and quickly got transported to a different world and time. I found myself immersed in her writing, in her stories. I read about her life as a child in Manchester, England, about her parents' decision to move the family from England to Canada, about arriving in Montreal and the poverty she and her family experienced, about the Jewish traditions that they lived according to, about her mother's death in their family home, and about her relationship with her father. I read about a lifetime of decisions that were born out of hardship and necessity, without the luxuries of choice, love, or money. I read about scarcity, suffering, adversity and, above all, the wisdom gleaned from a life that reads as anything but easy.

Celia Ploschansky-Deckelbaum's life in the early twentieth century was a stark reminder to me of how much abundance I had been born into, and, subsequently, how much I had taken for granted in my life. With the opening paragraph reading, "*This is the autobiography of my life, with some of my childhood experiences and memories, as far back as I can remember and the so many episodes and happenings that had occurred later on in my life. As this is like the re-opening up all the old wounds, I cannot shut the doors of my memories or forget the ones that I loved so deeply. This all happened so long ago, which makes me feel now as if I have finally come to the end of a sad and long journey, which would all go back to sixty-three years ago*", I knew without needing to read further that my own hardships and challenges would pale in comparison to what life was like for Grandma Simmie in those years.

I spent the next five days reading the autobiography cover to cover, forcing myself to pay attention and not glaze over or anesthetize through the more emotionally grueling passages. Reading about her mother's death in the family home shortly after she, Simmie, felt a sense of foreboding and dread,

"My Mother was lying in the centre of the dining room with a black cloth covering her for three days. I felt such an ache and void in my heart as I looked at her lying on the floor. She died at the age of forty-four, just two weeks after my sister's marriage."

Reading about how tight money was in the fallout of her mother's passing,

"As I felt so terribly alone, I found work in a sweater factory, which took an hours fast walking to work, and more than an hour walking back to my room, as I was too tired to walk fast. This factory is called "Knit To Fit" and still exists today. I started my days work in the morning at eight till six in the evening. After paying my rent I had next to nothing left. Gabrielle, who was teaching me French gave me each morning, a large square piece of home-made fudge, which sustained me for the day and on my way back, I bought some candy and a sour pickle on a side street for one cent. As time went on, I learned to live with all my inward pain which was stifled within me. I felt as if a whole area of my life was lost and missing. I enjoyed the sour pickle as I walked along, which was a real treat after all the sweet candy which I ate. I walked leisurely from work while looking in all the windows, seeing all the different displays on Ontario Street, as there was always something new to see in the windows. There were so many people passing by, which I found interesting, as everyone looked so different. As I looked at them, I kept wondering where they were all hurrying to, and where they all lived. I would at times come in very tired, and in my room just fall asleep with all my clothes on. In the morning I would splash some water on my face and walk to work. I knew that I was completely on my own and that I had to support myself in order to keep body and soul together."

Reading about how she found (false) solace in seeing her children leave home as they found their own way in life,

"I kept thinking that if the children went their own way, I would still have my husband who would never leave me, as we had been

through so much together. At this time, my husband was looking for a large space in a building, as he wanted to expand and add many more things and was very anxious to have the business out of the house. He had an appointment for eleven o'clock in the morning for the next day, with regards to a space. He was up early and as usual cheerful and full of hope. While eating his breakfast, he complained about not feeling well. I said, "Lie down on the couch and it will surely pass away." The couch was in the dining room, adjoining the kitchen, I was horrified to see him in a complete sweat. I telephoned our doctor, who came right away and had left a patient standing in his office. The doctor looked at him and said that he had a coronary thrombosis and doubted if he would come through. When the doctor and my son had left the room, I was alone with him and I could see him making an attempt to sit up, then he fell back. My daughter, Lillian, had gone quickly to the undertaker and had picked out the nicest coffin, which was all lined with white satin, as she said, "This is the last thing that Daddy will have." As I looked at him, I knew that he could not touch, see, or feel. All his hopes and inspirations had vanished into thin air to be nothing more than a few dull letters on a stone. As I was walking sadly upstairs to my room, I recalled how he had told me at one time, that as a child he and his family were bidden underground during a pogrom, while everyone around had been slaughtered. He had weathered many storms, as just being alive was an achievement. He was courageous, daring and not afraid of hard work, as our love for the children was beyond reason. At four in the afternoon, he was at the undertaker."

If the purpose of this book, the one you are reading right now, is to inspire and awaken the reader to recognize commonality using the stories that, once woven together, form the fabric of not only my narrative, but all of our narratives, then know that I am sharing my great-grandmother's because at the moment in time when I was finally ready to read and absorb it, it did just that for me. It reminded me that life can get difficult, plagued by economic hardship, loss, fear, and even plagues themselves. And Simmie herself reminded me, through words that have bridged two centuries, that in the presence of all that could fell us, there is still wisdom, insight, hope, and, above all, love. And considering I finished reading it a week before the Covid-19 crisis kicked off in North America, the commonality I found prepared me, in some queer way, to welcome and roll with Pandemica better than I think I would have had I not had her stories to refer back to.

I have included excerpts from her story because the story of Bram is greatly impacted by the stories of my family, my ancestry, the culture I was born into, and what I inherited from all of that. I grew up in the Jewish religion and culture, albeit very reform in terms of adherence to rituals and practices. My parents brought my two brothers and myself to synagogue on the High Holidays, experiences which I unconsciously was expecting to find value in, but in which I only found a superficial social opportunity for people to discuss their (and their family members') achievements, acquisitions, and social standing. The amount of materialism and small talk really irked me, even from a young age, because I, on some primal level, wanted to find something spiritual and God-like in that hallowed space of prayer. I also found the ritualistic choreography of call-respond-stand-sit impersonal and cultish, and quickly took the initiative, as previously mentioned, to bring books with me to prop up behind the prayer book. If everyone else was showing up for the sake of appearance, I was happy to do the same.

With that said, I went to a Hebrew primary school and was subsequently exposed to an education in Judaism and the oppression, discrimination, hatred, and genocide inflicted on the global Jewish community throughout history. Being exposed to films like *Shoah* in the later stages of my primary education was traumatic, to say the least. I now consider myself to be a lapsed Jew, non-observant and barely interested in paying attention to any religion, including Judaism, that serves to divide and classify humanity. I would be lying, however, if I said that my Judaic upbringing did not leave inherited, archetypical traces that still invisibly trail behind me to this day, outsider / victim / oppressed / rebel / underdog / fringe / unwanted / unheard / disposable traces that inform my life story, my life script, my narrative. My penchants for rejecting any voice of authority, having a very "fuck-you-very-much" kind of attitude, feeling like I will accomplish what I want and need to regardless of what other people think, teaching myself how to do what needs to get done in order to build my life and career according to my own expectations and standards, and often feeling rage bubbling under the surface at the slightest nuance of injustice, all, I believe, stem from those archetypical traces. I believe that much of what has informed my narrative and my story stems from a history and ancestry of legacy burdens. Legacy burdens are the cultural, emotional and systemic burdens that get passed down from generation to generation. It is no surprise that this peripatetic, homosexual, English speaking, fallen Jew living in a primarily heterosexual world and French-speaking province is ready to up sticks and move anywhere in the world at the drop of a hat. The irony that my life résumé shows decades-long commitment to jobs, relationships, and friendships, and that I have never lived in any other city than my city of birth, is not lost on me. But trust me, I could easily grab the essentials and get the hell out of dodge in a matter of hours if need (or want) presented itself. The feeling of being an "other", as well as the belief that I, and only I, can be depended on for my survival is deeply rooted in me. But what I carry with me is not all burden, trust me.

A character trait that I have inherited is a "fuck-you-very-much" attitude which I have referred earlier in the book, and that comes directly from my father. One story that has been passed down about my dad involved him in a restaurant bathroom peeing at a urinal. When he was finished and had zipped up his trousers, he started to walk out of the bathroom and was interrupted by another gentleman present in the room who asked him condescendingly, "Did your mother not teach you to wash your hands after you pee?" My father, without blinking, responded, "My mother taught me not to piss on my hands", and continued exiting the bathroom. Now *that* is my kind of badass.

Another moment with my father that will always stay with me dates back to the early 2000's. I was in his car with him and casually mentioned how I wanted to visit my friends in England, but that money was tight. I had always been worried about money and felt what I now understand to be an ancestral, unhealthy shame related to spending money on myself solely for pleasure instead of piling it up "just "in case", and so it was a big deal for me to consider spending a couple of thousand dollars on the trip. I should also mention that I did not have the money to spend. The cost of the trip would have gone directly to my credit card which was already close to maxed out.

My dad replied, simply and directly, "Go. Go to England", and with those three words, he taught me. He reinforced to me that there will always be reasons to justify not doing what we would like to, that there will never be enough money, enough time off, enough opportunity, and that we can either buy into that scarcity mindset or we can live our lives fully and enjoy the ride from a place of *carpe diem*, a place of abundance, a place of just-do-it/live-your-life - ness. He taught me that there will never be a perfect time. I ended up going on that trip, and I had the time of my life and did not suffer financially or otherwise because of it. He taught me what, essentially, is a teaching that stems from the First Noble Truth of Buddhism, which tells us that every human life will include suffering. No human being is exempt from suffering at various points in life. Knowing this to be true and inevitable, we are taught that our happiness cannot be contingent on external factors magically aligning so that we get whatever desired outcome we hope for or for the perfect opportunity to present itself. We are taught that it is up to every one of us to find that happiness in a world and existence replete with suffering, a world and existence in which there will never be a perfect time unless we make it a perfect time. My dad taught me to make it the perfect time, and to use whatever resources I had at my disposal to live my life the way I wanted to. To enjoy my time, even in the presence of that which would ordinarily have diverted me away from happiness. My dad the Buddhist. Who would've thunk?

Discussing my family without including my father's mother into the narrative would be irresponsible of me. From what I have gathered throughout the years of family stories passed down, my paternal grandmother's life was heavily tinged by mental illness. *The Book of Ruth*, which is how I refer to her narrative, as her name was, and always will be, Ruth, is a somewhat unforgiving one. Ruth apparently suffered from heavy bouts of depression as an adolescent, an illness that surreptitiously kept a grip on her throughout the rest of her life. Ruth was Hollywood gorgeous, in the vein of Rita Hayworth and Lauren Bacall, and the mythology handed down to her grandchildren includes her having dated Cary Grant.

The Book of Ruth recounts her meeting her future husband, Leon Levinson, and staying at the Levinson family house in Montreal when she visited from her native Toronto. Leon's parents and sisters disapproved of his glamourous girlfriend and apparently began a systematic mission to break her down with various forms of psychological torture, including going for "walks" with her to the Mount-Royal cemetery and then leaving her there to find her way back amid the gravestones and mausoleums. Another story tells of Ruth coming down for breakfast glamorously made up, ready for her day, at which point her new mother-in-law yanked her by the hair, shoved her head under the kitchen faucet, turned on the water full-blast and told her that she refused to have a whore in the house and to never show her face in full makeup like that again. Whether these stories are factual or not almost seems irrelevant at this point in my life, because what bleeds through the tales is the fragility of a woman left to fend for herself in a literal and metaphorical house devoid of love.

What I remember of Ruth is that she always seemed to have an Elizabeth Taylor-like filter enveloping her, as if she showed up in the world from behind a soft glow. She was always made up, hair and nails done, and she loved me with a purity and ferocity that speared its way through my childhood protection devices and left me feeling like there was someone else on my side. There was always a thin veil of sadness about her, a sadness that I recognized and was used to as well, and I have always felt that Ruth and I embodied a sensitivity that, in the hands of the wrong company, could be used against us. And despite Ruth having done serious psychological and emotional harm to her children and their spouses, because she never hurt me directly, because I always understood where her dysfunctional behaviour and occasional triangulation tactics stemmed from, I always only saw her as an injured, abused, abandoned soul. This empathy is not, I am sure, shared by her children or their other halves, and perhaps in the recounting of her narrative I am guilty of romanticizing a lifetime of irresponsible parenting and psychological abuse. Regardless, when I look back on old family photos and videos, I do not see an evil woman. I see someone who was born in the wrong century, at a time when mental illness had not been normalized into the collective conversation, who instead of being nurtured and accompanied throughout her illness, was strapped to a gurney at the Allen Memorial Psychiatric Hospital and given electric shock treatments to snap her out of her depressive and manic phases. I think of Ruth and want to hold and protect the child who grew into the woman who, for better or for worse, raised my father into the man who I love with all my heart.

With all that family history of struggle and strife, when I compare my experiences and history to Ruth's and to my maternal great-grandmother Simmie's as recounted by her in her autobiography, I recognize that my life has been, and continues to be, blessed. Having people to tell me that I was ok, and that life would be ok in the ways that I needed to hear may have been in short supply, and what I have inherited from those who came before me may just be normalized trauma, but know I have had it good. I had the luxury of navigating the struggles life had in store for me in a household where I never needed to question where the next meal was coming from or where I would be laying my head down to sleep every night. My parents parented. They always have, being particularly aware of when they could have abdicated leadership and put me or my brothers into the role of the caregiver, and intentionally going the opposite route. My father devoted himself to work, my mother did as well, and ensured that their children's existence and life choices were not born out of necessity or scarcity, unlike Simmie's or Ruth's were, and thereby changed key aspects of the legacies that had been handed down to them.

We could all do well to pay attention to the teachings which have been passed down to us by those who have come before us, especially those who have known and survived hardship. Simmie's words which close out her memoirs is just that, wisdom for the ages, wisdom that could only be born from the lived experience of the tales that make up the narrative.

"Time is fleeting and the years have passed like falling leaves. As we grow older we are not bound by conventions. Age has its compensations. We are reconciled to what we are and do not wish to impose with false pretences. I can remember how a look or glance would brand themselves eternal, how a careless word would linger. Today, wrapped up in the armour and composure of age, the everyday pricks brush me but lightly and are soon forgotten."

"Negative thoughts can be destructive if we let them get out of hand. J know that there are some things in life that we cannot forget, such as the death of someone that we loved and was part of us, which at times will stir within us und become suddenly alive. We must realize that everything that happens is natural and part of life. People in general are like baffled children as life is unpredictable. Many of us have gone through the valley of tears and bear within ourselves scars of many lost battles. We must remember that suffering is not completely lost as we gain a beauty of outlook, a philosophy of life and understanding, a forgiveness of humanity. In short, a quality

of peace and serenity. Time at last to explore the best and deepest part of human nature. I cannot help thinking that life is similar to a dream. So many things that were vital and of importance have all passed away."

"Nothing is more important than this day, as we cannot relive yesterday and tomorrow is still beyond our reach. As we grow older we should learn to make the most of each day. And so the world goes on endlessly, regardless of everything, as the best years which consist of childhood and youth just slips by, which is the common lot of all humanity, as we all come into the world alone and depart the same way."

After decades of struggling with life's inherent misfortunes and miseries, Grandma Simmie's words of insight and wisdom remind me, and us all, that the journey of life will always be strewn with hardship and despair, but that we must not get so caught up in the negative that we lose sight of the gifts suffering brings. If this experience of life is truly about transcending suffering in the presence of everything that could pull us further into it, then her words serve as an important reminder: when tiptoeing through the echoes of yesterday and the hardships of today, the life lessons that only suffering can produce are the jewels in the mud, waiting to be unearthed and appreciated so life can be appreciated and lived bigger than anyone has encouraged us to do. What her words also convey to me is that poverty, struggle, abandonment, turmoil, and despair are not the only legacies I have trailing behind me in my family history. Storytelling, love, inspiration, and recognition of it all as, in its most simple form, a story, also abound, and to not be aware of that would be to dishonour the lessons all the relatives who have come before me were blessed with, without whom these words would not exist.

THE LEGACY TEACHINGS CONT'D

When I had just entered my teen years, I went to spend a week in Florida with my mother's parents, Papa Mac and Mama Lil, Lil being Lillian, Simmie's daughter who picked out her father's coffin at the undertaker's when she was a little girl. As an adult, my grandmother was one of the first female real estate agents in Montreal, and despite having grown up in poverty, she earned her way into financial independence and stability. On that journey, she and her husband Max bought a modest, two-bedroom condo in Hollywood, Florida where I would go once a year, usually with a brother or a parent. I went to spend some quality time with them that year on my own, and quality was what I got.

I slept on the sleeper sofa in the living room while there and would get woken up every morning by my grandmother who would walk into the living room wearing her nightgown, her terrycloth hair towel and an inch of moisturizing cold cream smeared on her face. She would walk quickly into the room, leaning forward as she came to smother me in kisses and hugs, calling my name and laughing because she knew that I would pull away for fear of getting covered in her moisturizer. The love that she had for me was next level, and she made sure to know I felt it through so much of what she did and said.

I had a friend from elementary school who was also in Florida, staying at her parents' condo just down the road from my grandparents' place, who came over one afternoon for a hangout. As we watched TV and chatted in one room, Mama Lil went about preparing sandwiches for our lunch in the kitchen. She soon called us to come get the food, and when we walked into the kitchen, there she was, my lovely grandmother, standing next to the kitchen table, one sandwich plated and ready, the other one under a layer of tinfoil on the ironing board being pressed into a panini by the scalding hot iron. I suppose that the looks on our faces communicated incredulity because she looked at us and said matter-of-factly, "My sandwich press is in Montreal, so I got creative." Her resourcefulness that day was first met with embarrassment on my part, but that moment stuck in my mind and often ended up inspiring me to get creative when I found myself in uncertain situations later in life. The sandwiches were incredible, by the way, and that story survives to that day as a talking point with that friend whenever we cross paths.

As mentioned earlier, the mall was the greatest place to be back in the eighties, but nothing was cooler than a mall in the USA. Malls back home were great, but having access to American record and toy stores as a kid was the ultimate in bliss for me. When Mama Lil mentioned that she needed to go to the Aventura Mall, and would I like to come, I almost literally jumped up and down with excitement. She had once told me that she had observed how I had a tendency to spend money before I even had it, a tendency she wanted me to be aware of in order to, in her words, "understand the value of a dollar". And she was not wrong, especially that day she invited me to Aventura. I had been fixated on the new Billy Idol compilation album, *Vital Idol*, and I wanted to get the cassette version that day. The problem was that I had no money.

As I walked with her to the car on the way to the mall, she asked me if there was any store in particular I wanted to go to while there. I remember hemming and hawing, eventually mentioning that I wanted to go to the record store. I was walking next to her, hunched over staring down at the sidewalk as I mumbled, inwardly battling between wanting to ask her to buy me the cassette and wanting to say nothing as I anticipated her telling me it would be a waste of money. All of a sudden, she stopped walking and stopped me by putting one hand on my shoulder. Holding me in place, she took her other hand, balled it into a fist and pressed the middle knuckle into my curved spine until my spine lengthened and I was standing up straight looking at her. "Stand up straight", she told me, "Look people in the eyes, and don't ever be afraid to ask for what you want because no one is going to do it for you."

I will never forget that moment. While it may seem like she was meting out some harsh discipline, there was nothing harsh at all about it, just some loving advice that she felt was appropriate in the moment. She made it a teaching moment. We continued heading to the mall and I spent the rest of the week in Florida listening to Billy Idol.

Mama Lil was not only disciplined with money, but she was also incredibly so with food. Often plagued with leg discomfort due to her diabetes, she was hypervigilant about sugar, salt and unhealthy food. I remember her making lunch another day during that week in Florida, boiled chicken with green beans. The chicken was indeed boiled, served on a plate with no trimmings or sauces, bland as could be. That was how she rolled, preventatively controlling what she (and we) ate at the expense of any food-related enjoyment. One of the only luxuries in that condo was a bowl of sugar-free candy. I can still hear the crinkle of the cellophane wrapping as I popped a lemon-esque sweet into my mouth, only to find my jaws locked together when I unthinkingly bit down on it. I do not know what sugar substitute those candies were sweetened with, but I suspect that NASA might be familiar with it.

On her deathbed, when pancreatic cancer was draining the life out of her and her appetite was nearly nonexistent, the one thing she craved, and which my mother went to get for her, was a hamburger. And it was at that time that she admitted that she had been wrong, that she should have found more joy in her food instead of being so watchful over every meal and snack. I will always carry that wisdom with me, the knowledge that food is meant to be a source of joy, not only a means to a caloric end.

Mama Lil's husband, Papa Mac, had more of a quiet, unassuming character, and he loved her with a passion and devotion that really became apparent after she had passed away. After that, all he wanted was to be reunited with her in death. He waited eight or nine years to do so, but when he was done waiting, he decided that that was it. He had had enough of old age, once telling me that "getting old is not for sissies" and decided to just stop eating. Living in an assisted-living facility and seeing the world pass him by outside his room held no meaning for him at the ripe, old age of ninety-two, and so he just stopped eating.

Between that time and the time of his passing, his ninety-third birthday rolled around and my mother and one of her brothers (the other one was living in Mexico at the time) decided that we should all get together as a family and hold a birthday party for him. Sounds like a lovely idea, right? I certainly thought so, right up until the day of the party itself.

My mother brought my older brother, my partner and myself along with her in her car. My older brother had always been very careful with germs and not getting sick, so knowing he was coming along was something of a win. My mother drove her car into the basement garage of the assisted-living facility, and we made our way from the parked car to the elevator. When it arrived and the door opened, there was a nurse standing behind an elderly wheelchair-bound patient in the middle of the small space, at which point my brother said, "We'll take the next one!" I started giggling then and there. When the next elevator showed up, much to his relief, it was totally empty, so we got in and pressed the button for the third floor. When our ascent was interrupted by a stop on the first floor, I knew things were heating up. The doors opened and a nurse walked in, and then turned around and pushed us all against the elevator walls with her ample butt. I looked over at my brother, the side of his face nearly pressed up against the elevator wall, and I started losing my composure. We made it up to the third floor where we extracted ourselves and stopped to get our bearings as we looked for Papa Mac's room. The scene that we found ourselves in was like something out of The Simpsons. We were standing in the middle of the dining area where a guy in his forties was seated playing a synthesizer, singing along to "Michael Row Your Boat Ashore" with a handful of the elderly residents. I could feel my brother's discomfort as if I were some sort of emotional Geiger counter, which only added to my own. We started walking down a hall, soon finding my grandfather's room. And when we walked in ready for a party, we realized what we had signed up for.

Papa Mac was lying in bed, eyes closed, mouth agape as if he was taking his last breath. He looked dead. I was not actually sure if he was still alive but decided it was too distasteful to approach the subject, so we stood around chatting until my uncle arrived with his two daughters. As everyone took their coat off, we each said hi to Papa Mac, acting as if his non-responsiveness was the most normal thing in the world. They had brought dinner, bags of smoked meat sandwiches and other deli delights which we unbagged and plated. Out of nowhere, a disembodied voice feebly called out, "I love you, daddy". I looked around to see where it had come from, at which point my mother informed me that her brother in Mexico was with us via Skype on a laptop that was directed at my grandfather. That voice repeatedly popped up throughout the evening randomly, David Lynch-style. My father sat down in the power electric chair that my grandfather usually sat in, unaware that he was sitting on the button on the control panel. I stared in silence as my father bit into his sandwich, all the while slowly being tilted forward as the seat of the chair lifted. When he finally did realize, he started sputtering, "What – what the hell?" to which I replied, "Dad, you're sitting on the controls." He stood up, laughing uncomfortably, and found somewhere else to sit.

After dinner came the birthday cake. My mother put candles on the cake (not ninety-three of them, mind you), lit them and carried the cake towards Papa Mac as we all sung "Happy Birthday" in earnest (my uncle in Mexico's warbled Skype voice added the perfect tone of surrealness). I honestly do not remember who blew out the candles, but I sure as shit know it was not Papa Mac. We divvied up the cake, ate it, and then I got up and said to my partner that it was time to go. I actually felt like it was past time to go, that the whole situation should have never happened, that what we had done in the name of celebrating was actually a stain of shame on the family, but I kept that to myself. We said goodbye quickly to everyone and darted out of the room, and much to my relief, the dining area singalong was long over and done with. As we were waiting for the elevator, I said to my partner, "We shall never speak of this again". The Larry David-ness of the whole scene, the awkward cringe of continuing on with it when we all knew that despite the best of intentions, the party was not appropriate to Papa Mac's state, was all abrasively real to me.

My perspective on the birthday party changed as I got more distance and time from it. I realized that it had nothing to do with celebrating the patriarch of the family, quite the opposite, actually. His role in the whole equation was spookingly evocative of his actual participation in the occasion, meaning that he was the reason we came together as a family despite not having any input or involvement from him. The party was not actually for him at all, it was for us. It was an opportunity for us to use him as the excuse to gather, something we had done up to that day on every Jewish holiday and for every birthday party. Papa Mac was the one for whom all of that was important, and we kept it going right up until that birthday party. That was the last one. The last one for us, and the last one for him. When he passed away, so did the practice of coming together as a family, and I wish I had had the awareness then to recognize what I now can. But at least I figured it out. I now acknowledge the importance of every occasion we get as a family to gather, even the funerals which can be cherished as opportunities to reconnect to the familial ties that bind us all together.

What family teaches us is irreplaceable. We learn what to incorporate, what to steer clear of, what to file under "For future contemplation", and what to laugh ourselves silly over. The legacies we carry with us may occasionally feel like heavy burdens, absolutely. But when we understand the generations' worth of truth and life that are handed down to us through the accident of lineage and the sheer acts of interaction and accompaniment, we recognize that we serve as the living repository for those who came before us, for those without whom we would not be, for those without whom these stories that serve to inspire and unite would not exist. Their stories become ours, and ours become each other's once shared. That is what we are actually experiencing in life, connection born of the accumulation of generations of stories. What rich, abundant lives we lead.

ITHACA

I have always felt like I was in a race against time. Maybe it is that nomadic, never-get-comfortable legacy burden stemming from Judaism that has always had a hold on me, but regardless, it has always been there, for as long as I can remember. As a kid I wanted out of childhood and into adulthood as fast as possible. I did not relate to kids my age or younger, always finding that the people with whom I could have meaningful conversations and exchanges were always older. My friends when I was entering my teens were always at least four years older than I was, and where they went, I went, whatever they did, I did. I smoked cigarettes and drank alcohol as if I a) liked doing so, and b) knew what I was doing. I pretended I was in on the jokes and could completely relate when talk of sex arose, and I bought a fake identification card from some dodgy company that I found advertised in the classified section of an American tabloid newspaper. I remember being in Los Angeles while at a traveling summer camp in 1989, sealing the envelope into which I had placed a twenty-dollar bill along with a head shot of me taken at a photo booth in a mall, and voilà, six weeks later, once back home, I received the card in the mail that I confidently whipped out when I got asked to prove my age at one of the many bars or clubs my friends and I went to.

I believe that cultural and societal norms encourage us to focus on the future instead of taking pleasure and stock in the present. We are told that we need to have money in the bank and then invest it as we plan for retirement, and can I just take a quick moment to mindfully scoff at every financial advisor who told me that if I started investing twenty-five dollars every two weeks into a retirement fund from the age of twenty five, I would have one million dollars by the time I was sixty-five? What a bunch of commission-yearning charlatans and liars, but I digress. We are taught to look forward to the weekend or the next chunk of vacation days to relax and enjoy life. We are conditioned to accept that life will be better, that *we* will be better, when we have lost or gained whatever physical weight is required to mimic the aesthetic that the hive mind has accepted as worshipable. We fall for the commonly accepted fallacy that life will be better when whatever object of attention everyone else thinks is valid and of value is bought, achieved, consumed, attained or accomplished. That is when life will be great, when people will love us, when we will finally be good enough. That is when we will get what we assumed we would be rewarded with for playing the game of life according to the rules that others created long ago, many of which no longer apply in today's world, and which have not done for longer than many of us would be comfortable admitting.

As a child, I fell into the trap of believing that I had to be what I was not in order to be accepted, an imagined, idealized potential future version of myself. Bram 2.0. I believed I needed to be heterosexual, less sensitive, more emotionally resilient, a better athlete, dumber in certain moments and smarter in others, taller, more masculine, more muscular, less analytical, more of a doer and less of a thinker. I was always in a rush to become someone else, and lord help me if I received positive reinforcement in my attempts to be different, because that encouraged me to keep going with a renewed vehemence and intensity. If I got compliments related to whatever I was trying to enhance or project, always with the intention of deflecting attention away from what I believed I lacked, it fueled me to continue down the path of inauthenticity and build barriers between the truest aspects of myself and the rest of the world. But if I got called out and othered when I was just being myself? Disaster.

I remember being at a friend's house with his sister during my elementary school years. We were in their kitchen getting something to drink, and my friend poured himself a glass of Coca-Cola and topped it off with some water. I had never seen anyone do that with Coke, and I exclaimed, "Diluted Coke? Wow! That's crazy!" His sister looked at me like I had just grown a tail and said something to the effect of, "Diluted? Who uses words like that? What the hell kind of thing is that to say?"

I will never forget how hurt I was, how attacked I felt in a moment when I was so comfortable and open and just having a good time. My painful shyness as a kid always betrayed me in moments of feeling exposed by manifesting as blushing. I can still, to this day, remember the flush of the heat starting in my chest and quickly creeping up my neck to engulf my head and my face. I would turn purple, sweating, heart pounding, feeling betrayed by my body's inability to hide my feelings to whoever I was with when it occurred. I remember it happening at that moment, as the realization that I was being seen and branded as a freak because of a word that I used, and ultimately, because of my intelligence. I remember feeling like I wanted to return the hurt, volley it back to her so she could feel a fraction of what I was feeling, make her feel horribly as well, but I kept my mouth shut, as I just wanted to get out of their home and go back to the comfort of mine. And trust me when I say that all I wanted after that comment was to grow up, grow out of being the kid who was strange and overly mature and used words like "diluted", and get to the good stuff in life that I desperately hoped was in store for me. Little did I know that what I was yearning for was accessible in that very moment of feeling freakish, belittled, devalued. All I needed to do was assert and defend myself, believe in myself as I was instead of how I dreamed myself to be, to recognize the value and beauty in that wordy little nerd whose languaging spoke to his education and his ability to express his thoughts efficiently and maturely. It took me another decade to figure it out but figure it out I most certainly did.

Life is about owning, respecting and honouring who you are faster and quicker than normally occurs when you have to slog through everyone else's opinions and projections. In my rush to get to the magical life phase of "easy", I felt like I was rushing to get to my own unique experience of home, Odysseus-like, in which life would be better than it had been. What I have since learned is that I was indeed rushing to get home, but it was not the nostalgia-tinged home I grew up in, nor was it an abstract home in which everything would be lollipops and shooting stars, but rather a home I grew to understand as existing within myself, the home of me as me, as I was, comfortable and confident in my skin. Home was a state of mind in which I could finally understand that that version of me, with everything that had gotten put under the microscope and been made to feel valueless, was not only brilliant, but worth defending, standing up for, fighting back for, and recognizing as sacred in its uniqueness. I have learned that defining my worth and value based on other people's opinions is a dangerous game. After all, if I believe them when they love me, I will believe them when they don't. If I had understood back then that there was only one of me in all of time, replete with all of the idiosyncrasies, sensitivities, quirks, and foibles, perhaps I would have then understood how precious and miraculous the me-ness was. Instead, I looked to what the bullies and the cool people did, what they said, how they behaved, how they ran and played sports and socialized and smiled and treated others and decided to negate my me-ness and take a page from their books instead of realizing the classic-ness of my own volume.

When I look back at that old version of me through the lenses of experience and awareness, I want to protect that boy with every ounce of energy and fight I have in me today. I want to tell him that his suffering is not simply the cross he has to bear through a shitty life of hardship and inequality. I want to tell him that the proclivity he had to walk around quietly humming the songs that were in his head was not just another sign of being weird but was an actual, proven way to stimulate the parasympathetic nervous system to bring about sensations and feelings of calm and safety, and he came up with that on his own. I want to tell him that every second of the experience of feeling inferior and an afterthought, unwelcome and uninvited, is a rite of passage. I want him to know that every second of adversity and perseverance is a second closer to his rebirth and surfacing. I want him to know that this me-ness we share, this sensitivity and ability to empathize, this ability to see past the noise we all launch at each other and identify the humanity which lies beneath, this Benjamin Button-ness that had us wiser and more emotionally aware than the world and culture around us thought we should be at that young age, this was our True North, our North Star, our path of dharma, our *raison d'être*. I want to tell him that through this rebirth, this phoenix-from-the-flame process, he will emerge qualified and educated by the higher education life had in store for him. I want him to know that this life education, this Higher Learning, will qualify and certify him to accompany others through their dark nights of the soul. I want him to know how it will all help others to recontextualize their struggles and suffering, to inspire them to persevere and reclaim their power, to rise again and shed their skins of uncertainty, disillusionment, and hopelessness.

I now know, with every fiber of my being, that in order to find my power, certainty in my path, and my complete and utter rejection of anyone else's opinion or suggestions for what was right for me, I needed to suffer enough to finally be sick of it and choose another path. Instead of continuing to invalidate what made me myself, I would, with the most punk rock of attitudes, celebrate and understand its glory until the rest of the world woke up to what I had finally figured out. I needed to be reborn through my angst and fear and recognize that whole age of fuckery as a rite of passage leading me to rebirth, reinvention, rediscovery, reconstitution. This rite of passage was not and is not relegated solely to me. This is everyone's right of passage into finding that ever-elusive missing life link.

With all of that said, despite having figured out that everything that contributed to the Bram-ness was not only valid, but pretty incredible, the pattern of seeking worth and validation from what was outside of me had established itself as a habit. Over the next few decades, I became that guy who looked for the next home, the next opportunity, the next gadget, the next acquisition, believing that in achieving and amassing what I placed value on, I would somehow attain what I was seeking as a child: worth, acceptance, respect, love, and good-enough-ness. What I eventually gleaned was that regardless of whatever I succeeded in achieving or obtaining, I had become addicted to the chase. When what had previously been desired became actuality, its worth and ability to assign worth faded, and I would find myself resetting my sights on the next seemingly impossible task or acquisition that would be, *could* be, the thing that I believed would allow me to finally sit back, relax, pat myself on the back and finally feel good enough.

This pattern manifested one year when I was in Greece giving the annual Yoga and Meditation Vacation. I decided that I needed to start looking for a home to buy on the island, despite not having the money to buy one outright. I felt like I needed to put the feelers out, see what the market was like, meet with real estate agents and get the ball rolling on something that seemed impossible, hence desirable.

I spoke to Stella, my business partner and the owner of the hotel where our groups always stayed and told her that I was interested in looking into properties on the island. She told me she could arrange to have a real estate agent meet me and take me around the island, and I told her I would let her know what day during my stay would be most opportune to make it happen. I never got back to her on the subject. With my days occupied with the group and the activities we did together, I never got around to it. I talked about it, yearned for it, but did not make it happen. At the end of my stay that year, after hearing me incessantly express my goal of owning a home there, Stella presented me with a handwritten note, a transcribed and translated excerpt from the poem *Ithaca* written by the Egyptian-Greek poet Constantine Cavafy in reference to Homer's *The Odyssey*, the tale of Odysseus' struggle to get back home to the island of Ithaca following the Trojan War in *The Iliad*. Here is the excerpt of the poem that Stella transcribed for me,

"When you set out on your journey to Ithaca,
Pray that the road is long,
Full of adventure, full of knowledge…

Always keep Ithaca in your mind.
To arrive there is your ultimate goal.
But do not hurry the voyage at all.
It's better to let it last for many years,
And to anchor at the island when you are old,
Rich with all you have gained on the way,
Not expecting that Ithaca will offer you riches.

Ithaca has given you the beautiful voyage.
Without her you would have never set out on the road.
She has nothing more to give you.
And if you find her poor, Ithaca has not deceived you.
Wise as you have become, with so much experience,
You must already have understood what Ithaca means".

– Constantine Cavafy (1911)

I was so moved by the gesture, by Stella taking the time to write out the excerpt of the poem for me as a piece of guidance on my own journey, a piece of advice telling me to slow down, to remember that the journey is what matters, the destination only a beacon drawing me in a specific direction in which my narrative awaited. It took me years of having that letter from Stella to fully understand that it was ok to let go of the incessant wanting that always had me seeking the next mark of potential approval and affirmation. My own personal True North went from being pointed outwards, towards achieving and conquering, to finally, after four decades of running, being pointed internally towards myself, where I was, how I was, with nothing to change, nothing to fix, nothing to acquire, nothing to improve upon. All because of my own Greek goddess, business partner, friend, and chosen family member. I will always be indebted to Stella for planting the seed of wisdom in my heart and my mind. In her quiet, poetic, wise way, she became one of The Keepers for me. In sharing that poem with me, she helped that vulnerable, miniature, immature version of me heal by getting a macro view of my past and recognize the race I had been running. She allowed that unsure, shy, sensitive boy to accept himself finally and fully, and to navigate the unseen and unheralded rite of passage into adulthood, years after the age of the body had, for all intents and purposes, reached it.

We constantly hear the tired cliché, "It's about the journey, not the destination." I have even written about it in books and articles, thinking at the time that I had completely understood the full extent of its teachings. But like most wisdom that leaks into the realm of greeting cards and memes, its implications continued to prove valuable across varying moments and contexts, reappearing this time as full-blown insight from the kindest soul in Greece. I no longer want that home in Greece. I now know that the home itself would not signify anything other than another set of walls with a roof in a different geographical location than the homes I have previously lived in. It would not define me, nor would it raise my metaphorical net worth. That worth exists regardless of the baubles and acquisitions that I pick up on my way towards Ithaca. I finally get it. And I hope you do too. All those things that captured my attention were simply doing so to school me in the concept of worth. I am my own Ithaca. And the journey, in its roundabout and winding way, was always bringing me back to me. Not an imagined future version of myself, but the me who existed in the now. Nothing to change, nothing to fix.

PARCE QUE JE PEUX

My hometown of Montreal is a French-speaking city, or more specifically, a Québécois-speaking city, and the slogan on the province of Quebec's license plates reads *Je me souviens* ("I remember"), a reference to the often-volatile history and survival of Quebec's culture. Years ago I ended up in a joking conversation about how the slogan should be changed to *Parce que je peux* ("Because I can"), referring less to the province's history and more to how Montreal drivers shun rules and get away with whatever they can, simply because they can.

That expression, "because I can", took on an entirely different meaning for me, however, after the first time I went to Western Canada to work. I was teaching five different modules throughout a weekend of workshops in British Columbia, and one of the attendees was a guy named Jim. Jim was a local in the small town I was teaching in, a guy who, decades earlier, had survived a car accident that had left him brain injured. The lasting effects of the accident that were evident included slurred speech as well as a gradual hunching over of his upper body as he walked, his upper body slowly leaning forwards and off to one side until he would lift himself back up vertically again. He was a really funny, personable dude who spoke openly about the accident and how it had changed his life.

Following the lunch break on one of the workshop days, Jim told me that he would be leaving the afternoon module early, as he wanted to go skiing at the nearby resort before sundown. I gave him the thumbs-up, at which point the woman seated next to him asked him, "Aren't you afraid of hurting yourself again?" I supposed that she was taking into consideration the injuries he had already survived in the car accident and the obvious challenges he had been dealing with ever since. Jim looked at her without blinking an eye and responded, "I am more afraid of not being able to do it." And in that moment, I recognized Jim not as my student *per se*, but as my teacher. I had shown up in that small town on the other side of Canada with the intention of teaching and had ended up learning a lesson that has stayed with me to this very day.

I had rarely considered what the experience of life might be like for someone who had once been fully abled in body and mind and who had lost that abled-ness. Like a person with sight who loses the ability to see and spends the rest of their time living as functional a life as possible, Jim schooled us that day. By conveying to us that the need to ski, to have the freedom to slide down the side of that mountain, to live life the way he wanted to, was stronger and more galvanizing than the fear associated to what might happen if another accident occurred, he taught us a fundamental truth. He conveyed to us that courage and the faith related to how things could go right was more powerful in his private logic than the fear of how things might go wrong. He gave us direct insight into the often-forgotten ability we all have to not only adapt to situations that could befall us, but to actually live with intention and thereby thrive in the face of adversity.

A few years later Jim's teaching integrated itself in the oddest of circumstances. I was going to teach a class for a company downtown, and as I got into the elevator which would bring me up to the eighteenth floor of the building we held classes in, two women also got into the elevator with me, deep in conversation. One of them was recounting to the other how her company had invited a public speaker to come to their office for some sort of Lunch and Learn presentation, and the speaker had kicked off his presentation by asking, "What do you know will never happen?". What followed, apparently, was a collective silence that was only broken by the speaker repeating the question. The woman recounting the story then asked the woman she was speaking to, "What kind of idiotic question is that? What do we know is never going to happen? How am I supposed to know what is never going to happen?" They both laughed at the perceived inanity of the question and of the presenter, oblivious to me standing behind them in the elevator, chomping at the bit to put in my two cents and answer the question for them. I, of course, said nothing, as the elevator got to my floor, but I felt so inspired by the question and the thoughts it provoked that I started the class I was there to teach by asking the students the same question, "What do you know will never happen?" Not surprisingly, I was met with fifteen or so pairs of eyes looking at me blankly, so I took the liberty to offer my insight, "What do we know is never going to happen? Well, there may be many things that we suspect will not occur for us, but generally speaking, I believe that it is safe to say that we know, with a good degree of certainty, that the majority of our fears and anxieties will most likely never happen. The things we obsess over, the worst-case scenarios that we go over and over in our mental meanderings, the things we are afraid of occurring, will most likely never happen."

And with that said, I could see the faces of the students light up with understanding and a degree of affirmation. We chatted about it for a bit before we sat for meditation, but I have never forgotten that overheard bit of wisdom, wisdom echoed by a quote from Mark Twain I had read years before, "I… have known a great many troubles, but most of them never happened", attributed to him in the April 1934 edition of *Reader's Digest*. The mind usually meanders along an uninterrupted loop of catastrophic *what-ifs*, when, in reality, most, if not all of them, will never come to pass. We stay stuck in the abstract, stuck in the fear of the *what-ifs*, all the while missing the *what-is*, oblivious to what is going on in real time around us.

Fear will always send us in the opposite direction of where we want to go. Understanding that the main factor that holds us back in the pursuit of that which we seek is the fear of how things might go wrong is paramount in recognizing that not only should we not allow fear to lead, but that we *can* and we *should* show up in every possible moment to make the most of that moment, to live as much life as possible, even when faced with impediments, physical or otherwise.

Jim had learned this lesson, and with that one comment he made between workshops in that room where I was working in the BC interior, he taught that lesson to the woman he was speaking with, to me, and to anyone else who was paying attention. Because of Jim's words, the meaning of the expression "Because I can" changed for me, initially referring to a motivator for questionable driving, but post-Jim, pointing me towards not taking anything for granted and making the most of life. "Because I can", obviously very similar to Barack Obama's 2008 presidential campaign slogan, also became the mantra I began to draw upon to access deeper reserves of energy and determination in all aspects of my life. From helping me stay more energized when writing this book to giving me the kick in the ass I often need when running or working out, Jim's words have constantly served as the reminder I needed, and that I believe we all need, to appreciate the blessings and to get things done (and life lived) with intention and vigor, especially when taking care of the aspects of daily life that feel more like a chore than a pleasure.

In the blink of an eye, circumstances can change, and along with it can change the freedom and ability we have gotten accustomed to. Even more simply put, the things that we do mindlessly under the assumption that they will always be available and possible could become monumentally more difficult, even impossible, if one tiny detail in our individual narratives were to change. I have learned that anything can happen to anyone at any time, and so Jim reminded me to not only be grateful and aware of the blessings that exist in my life that allow me to be able and independent, but to always do as much as I can to live my life the way I want to live it, even in the presence of the fears and more demotivating thoughts or circumstances. What a lesson. Do it because you can, and do not take the fact that you can for granted, because with the slightest twist of fate, that *can* might be transformed into a *cannot*. And don't ever doubt that even when, on the off-chance, some of those worst-case scenarios *do* come to pass, there will still be agency and choice. There will always be some way to practice the "because I can".

THE FLIGHTS OF THE FANTASTICAL

In England a while back, I spent some time with friends and their eight-year-old daughter who, as the adults sat around eating lunch, sat on the floor on the other side of the room in a world of her own. Sitting across from one of the family dogs, she was completely immersed in the fantasy that she had created, content as could be. She spoke to the dog as if in full conversation, explaining which toy was which as the dog's eyes followed her movements adoringly. I turned to the girl's mother and told her to foster that imagination, to recognize the value of her daughter's ability to have a party for one (two, if you count the dog), to encourage and steer it in the directions that felt intuitive for their daughter and for themselves. I was witnessing unfettered imagination being authentically expressed, something that, properly directed, could lead her to the most fulfilling and creative of futures.

Imagination and a mind tilted towards the fantastical are so important for me, and for all artists and creators. I have always been tuned into fantasy and imagination. In fact, in the mid to late seventies, as a young kid exposed to films and television series about aliens, creatures from other realms, and kids' shows like *Fraggle Rock* and *Sesame Street*, I would sit on the toilet in the bathroom down the hall from my bedroom and stare into the ventilation grate that came out of the floor. I had these three imaginary friends who peered at me through the vertical slats in the ventilation cover, three imaginary friends who just happened to look exactly like the Rice Krispie characters, Snap, Crackle & Pop. I, for some reason, named them Erks, Jerks, and Rahr. Don't ask me why. I don't know. Anyways, we would chat. And have full conversations. Other times, again sitting on the toilet (isn't this where we all do our best work?), I would mentally transport to being the guest on a talk show being interviewed. And I would talk about all the things that I had done that day, what I had accomplished, basking in the audience's applause and soaking up the excitement of being in-studio with the heat of the warm lights on my face, seated across from the talk show host. For real. All while sitting on the toilet. I loved those moments because it was in those moments that I felt engaged, connected, part of something dreamy and bigger than myself, and it was exactly that energy of engagement and connection I saw in my friends' daughter.

I believe that because I was enrolled in schools which killed imagination with rote memorization instead of fostering it, I had a tough time in later elementary school and most of high school. And because I went to that *Dead Poet's Society*-esque school where nurturance was absent and discipline was meted out in abundance, I survived some very formative years by quashing my imagination and doing what I needed to do to get by. Cut to starting college after being in that high school, being exposed to freedom when I had been in what felt like prison for five years, and quickly dropping out after realizing that I was being pathed down an avenue which would only lead to more conformity and little to no imagination or passion.

I struggled for the next few years, feeling let down by my family, society, and the educational system. I vacillated between trying to make school happen over and over again to getting whatever job I could while I metaphorically treaded water to keep up the appearance of being alright. In truth, I was just starving for someone to tell me I could relax, take my time, explore all options, and then figure out what I wanted to study and eventually try working in. I struggled throughout those years, and that struggle was evident to my parents who, I now believe, had absolutely no idea how to effectively accompany me through this.

Grasping at straws, my mother arranged for me to visit with one of her brothers who had done extremely well in business, hoping that maybe some of his entrepreneurial brilliance would rub off on me. I was uncomfortable going to meet him because I was essentially doing so carrying the weight of the loser archetype on my shoulders, the lost, the needy. But I went. And one thing he said to me that afternoon ended up sticking with me throughout my life, which was, "Whatever you do, make sure you are the best at it." I remember understanding the meaning and the value of his words, but also feeling even more lost because I had no clue as to what I could be the best at. I was the odd one out, largely because, unlike everyone around me, I had no motivation to make money, prioritizing instead my happiness and a path that would bring me purpose and spark inspiration and passion. I needed my imagination and creativity to matter if I was going to choose something to do with my time. Even back then, I always felt like I was in a race against time and wasting it was not an option. I would have rathered do nothing with my time, essentially allowing myself to play the failure in the eyes of everyone else who played the good, obedient game of life, then do anything that did not feel authentic or purpose driven.

I knew I was swimming against the current. I grew up among professionals. One grandfather a court reporter. One grandmother a pioneer in the real estate industry as one of the first women to venture into the domain. My father, uncles, cousins, all lawyers. My mother a travel agent, her brothers, both entrepreneurs. Compared to them, I felt like a massive failure. All I knew was that I had no idea what I cared enough about to spend my time doing in order to earn money and support myself throughout the rest of my life, while hopefully earning the respect of others in the process. My uncle's advice was a tough pill to swallow, but it did get digested, and it served as a catalyst for me to direct my fantasy and creativity-tilted mind towards possible scenarios and worlds in which I was the best at something. Over a decade later, when I finally chose my path instead of settling for the one that presented itself, I understood that his advice was telling me to be the best version of myself, to magnify and amplify what my strengths were, and turn those strengths into a life-long career. He was teaching me to be the best at being myself and in making my own way forward, not at being the best at something I could not have given two shits about. Through his words I learned to not give anything or anyone more power than I give myself, and that is a foundation to how I live my life today.

I believe that nurturing a fantastical and imaginative mind is essential, but like all things, moderation is also essential. Spending cognitive time in fantasy can have its drawbacks, ones that experience and studying mindfulness later in life exposed all-too harshly for me. The fantastical mind is one which is pointed towards the abstract, towards the past and/or the future, towards the imagined or remembered. I have learned, in the harnessing of the fantastical-pointed mind, that to find balance, one must bring one's mind back to where one's body is. I often say in classes and lectures that it does not matter where your body is, you are where your mind is. The evidence of this for me can be found in my childhood, when regardless of who I was with or where I was, my mind was immersed in make-believe and imagined realms. The shadow side of a fantasy-tilted mind kept me, and occasionally still keeps me, from being fully present and soaking up the totality of a moment. I believe that back then, being in those alternate headspaces was a survival technique that funnelled my creativity into feeling connection and engagement when my literal world lacked both those experiences. But what tends to happen is we bring our tactics along with us into adulthood, even when they no longer serve us as effectively as they once did. I have learned to distance myself from those tactics so I could break from the patterns of attaching to the belief that there is always something better available and lying in wait, something else to dream of, something new to fixate on, someone or something or somewhere or somehow newer and fancier and shinier and better and brighter. I can more easily come back to my "now" moment and find value then and there. We are constantly being sold the newest version of what we already have and are being conditioned that "newer" carries more worth, so breaking from my old beliefs and thought patterns was, and still occasionally is, a huge challenge, but practice does, indeed, make a huge difference.

It is not all fear and doom and gloom with my fantasy-tilted mind when it becomes untethered and left to lead. The tendency to romanticize what seems attractive long before it proves to carry value or worth has been a source of amusement for me and the stories I tell for a long time. The meaning and greatness that I have assigned to the most mundane of situations, romantic interests, friendships, and career opportunities because of my tendency to fantasize and romanticize is almost embarrassing and has produced the greatest (and most uncomfortable) stories, especially when it comes to dating and to shopping while on my travels.

When I was between relationships I had met someone online and had been chatting with them for a couple of weeks when we decided to meet up and have a proper date. Being the hopeless romantic I have always been, I decided that we should meet for dinner and then go see a film together. I chose *Amen*, a Nazi-themed war-drama directed by Costa-Gavras. I was completely sold on how we would meet at the restaurant; the sparks would fly and we would finish the date off on an intellectual note with the movie.

We met up at the restaurant as planned and sat down at our table, the conversation flowing easily. I found myself a little disappointed by his appearance, as he did not look precisely as he had in the photos he had shared with me, but not wanting to be completely superficial, I let go of any judgement and decided to let the evening progress naturally. The restaurant we had chosen was, and still is, a Montreal institution known for its multi-layered sandwiches, often slathered in thick layers of cream cheese or peanut butter. We ordered our meals and kept on chatting, but slowly began noticing that there was absolutely no chemistry, no spark of connection or interest for me. I noted the observation and let it go, still intent on being open and unattached to any narrative. We kept chatting until the waiter brought our food to the table, at which point events took an unexpected turn. As we prepared to tuck into the meal, he looked at me and told that I would need to excuse him as he needed to take his teeth out.

I am pretty sure that my face said everything that I withheld from speaking out loud because he went on telling me how he was about to have dental surgery to implant two teeth but that until then they needed to come out when he ate. He then proceeded to remove his incisors and place them on the napkin that was placed next to his plate of food. I can still see it: a triple-layered sandwich on brown bread slathered in cream cheese with a side salad arranged next to it, two teeth innocently placed on a thin paper napkin beside the plate. Between you and me, I remember hearing brakes squeaking in my mind, as if to say that this ride had just come to a screeching halt. I did my best to regain composure and carried on like nothing had happened, all the while mentally kicking myself for having arranged a film after the dinner when all I wanted to do was eat and get back home. Seeing as how I had not yet learned to speak up for myself and set boundaries, I kept mum on wanting to bolt and we went to watch the movie after dinner. That experience that can only be described as an exercise in trying to keep my hand as far away from his as possible, as he kept trying to hold my hand by brushing my pinky finger with his. As much as I felt badly that I was spurning his advances, I just wanted out. The whole evening was a lesson in not only managing expectations when all I wanted was to fall in love, but in also being a little more discriminating when it came to choosing first-date activities.

Now, when it comes to travel, I must mention how much I love being away and shopping in new stores with unique, different products. Travel brings new experiences, cultures, tastes, sounds, sights, smells, and sensations to my life, and during my travels, I used to buy things that I believed I would never find back home and, upon my return, would unpack with an air of victory. One might assume that these finds would have occurred in luxury shops or markets boasting antiquities and curiosities. One would be wrong. I usually found my treasures in supermarkets, drugstores and homeware stores. What can I say? I am a simple lad. And what have I brought back home, you ask?

Shopping in a homewares store in rural England, I came across a food scale boasting the best technology that 1950 could offer. An old-fashioned food scale with a round, chrome dish to put on top of the weighing mechanism, with that skinny red needle that rotates to indicate the weight of the food. And I could not get over how cool it was. I immediately began fantasizing about having it in my kitchen, of using it to weigh flour as I mixed ingredients together to bake bread (I had never baked bread before in my life). I felt like I had never seen anything like it before. So, I bought it. And I carried it home with me as carry-on luggage on the flight back, holding onto that cardboard box for dear life.

Another find which I stumbled onto in England was a peeler. You know that thing that is used to peel carrots, potatoes, etc.? It was clean and simple, stainless steel. And I was absolutely sold on it, visualizing how I would always use this revolutionary tool while romantically remembering buying it in this quaint, little shop.

In yet another charming English shop, I came across lime leaves, great for using in Thai soup and stir-fry recipes. I bought five packets of them, envisioning all the soup I would be making for my highly impressed and forever grateful friends. Once back home, I proudly showed them to a friend as if I had discovered actual gold, and was met with, "You can get these at the supermarket two blocks from here." She uttered the words between hysterical gasps for air as the tears of her laughter streamed down her face.

The mother lode of my forays in English supermarkets had me fixate on something called stock cubes. Stock cubes, I discovered, were compressed cubes of high-sodium, powdered stock meant to be diluted and used in recipes calling for vegetable, chicken, or beef broth. I was BLOWN. AWAY. I bought three packs. I could not believe the convenience of not having to lug around cartons of broth, instead having the space-efficient option of these flavoured nuggets. I brought them back home with me, desperate to show them off. I showed them to my partner as if I had unearthed a rare, prehistoric scarab from under the most innocuous of rocks. He looked at me as if he was truly seeing me for the first time in his life, a look glaringly tinged with disbelief. "Stock cubes? Are you being serious? You can get these at the supermarket across the street for a buck or two."

Allergy pills, garlic presses, toothbrush holders, a UK-region DVD player that would not function back home in Canada, shower gels (10 at a time, pushing my luggage past weight limits that then required me to pay even more to the airline), body moisturizers (further testing the weight limits of my luggage), spices, herbs, food, cologne, clothing, and books. I have bought products I was *sure* I could not find at home, immediately lost in the romanticized fantasy of being *that guy* who had stock cubes and was so ultra cool that I absolutely had to purchase them.

Lesson #1 from this whole shit-show? Don't underestimate globalization. Save your money when abroad, mindfully remembering that whatever it is you feel inclined to purchase is most likely available for less a few blocks away from home. Lesson #2? Wherever you are, and let me clarify, wherever *your body* is, bring your mind there and be fully and totally in that moment. And if that moment includes you being so enraptured by another culture and another place, enchanted by the miracle that you can enjoy the palate-pleasing wonders of broth without the hassle of lugging around 1-litre boxes of liquid (or whatever other novel discovery you come across), allow yourself to be in that space of marvel and buy allll the things that fulfil and anchor you into that moment in time. Forget Lesson #1. Live your allergy pill, garlic press, toothbrush holder, DVD player, shower gel, body moisturizer, spice, herb, food, cologne, clothing, book fantasy. And then carry that shit home in your overweight, over-paid-for luggage (or your hands, if you buy a food scale).

I know that the mind that tends towards the fantastical is one which is steeped in possibility, in which the most random of ideas could instigate the creation of a work of art or innovation that might inspire and uplift millions of people. Imagination and awareness of the powers of intention and creation is essential. We need to dream, to imagine, and we need creators and innovators, dreamers who spend cognitive time in the imagined and make it manifest. However, when untethered, that mind can bring us into some scary, destabilizing places (and some ridiculously funny ones in which questionable shopping might occur). A healthy dose of presence of mind peppered into the fantastical combined with a refusal to allow fear to motivate my actions has proven to be the recipe for thriving in my experience. This is a recipe we would all do well to master so we can let imagination and creativity rule and contribute to the world of inspiration and elevation that our world so desperately needs. As I will delve a little deeper into in the next chapter, fear has been an important obstacle in my life experiences and transcending that fear has not only been part of my life's work, but I believe the work we all need to do to finally dismantle the systems of impotence and scarcity we have allowed to lead for far too long.

JE SUIS CLINT EASTWOOD

Post-workout at the gym one Sunday morning, I went into the locker room and passed by a guy changing into his workout clothes a few lockers away from mine. I prepared to go shower, closed and locked the locker, but then realized that I had forgotten to put my water bottle inside it. Taking the lazy option, I placed it on the bench and went to shower. After showering I headed into the sauna to dry off and through the window in the door of the sauna, I saw the guy who had been changing into his workout clothes walk out of the changing room carrying his towel, his phone, and my water bottle. He had a totally neutral expression on his face, and *my* water bottle in his hand.

I immediately felt anger flare up, incredulous that I couldn't leave a simple, empty water bottle in a semi-public place for longer than five minutes before someone took it. I decided I wasn't going to rush my sauna experience because of him, that I would breathe deeper, calm my nervous system, take my time getting back to my locker, and get dressed without rushing. As I consciously breathed through my irritation to find some calm, I also began conjuring up my revenge. The plan was that I was going to get dressed, get my coat on, walk out of the locker room, find the guy in the gym, grab my water bottle from him and tell him in these exact words, "Don't steal other people's shit." I'd then walk away, deaf to whatever response he'd try to throw my way and leave, victorious, having stood up for everyone who had ever been slighted or wronged throughout history. I had it all planned. I was fired up, literally (from the sauna) and metaphorically.

I got out of the sauna, headed back to the showers to rinse off and then walked back to my locker. Where my water bottle was placed exactly as I had left it. There it was, intact, untouched, waiting patiently for me so it could remind me just how ridiculously lost I sometimes get in situations that are completely of my own imagining. This guy obviously had a bottle similar or identical to mine. I had assumed that he had taken mine, and I had conjured up this entire Game of Thrones, righting-the-wrongs-of-injustice-fueled scenario of indignation and confrontation based on nothing more than an assumption.

From the moment he had walked out of the locker room with what I had assumed was my bottle, I was wrong. Totally, unequivocally wrong. Regardless of how long I have existed in this body, regardless of whatever experience I may have amassed, regardless of what I think I know, my perception obviously fails me even in the most certain of moments. Yes, I am a human being with a human brain that can be regarded as a meaning-making machine, but it led me astray with the meaning that it assigned to the situation. I formulated opinions about what had happened and what this man was capable of doing, and I was wrong. Instead of responding to all the facts I would need to fully understand what was going on, I instead reacted emotionally to the conclusion I had jumped to. And if every experience has a lesson that can be gleaned from it, this one taught me that I need to continue working to deprogram initial response, regardless of how certain I may be about whatever situation I am involved in. It taught me that I should be questioning the conclusions and certainties I base opinions and actions on, knowing from experience that even when I am totally convinced about something, I can be embarrassingly wrong. It taught me to be ready for the next time an incident arises where I feel assumption and emotional reaction flare up. It taught me to witness the response, take a deep breath, and consider that there is most likely another explanation to be gleaned, and then gather the evidence I need to actually know what I am dealing with instead of running on the fumes of supposition.

Cut to a few months later and I am back at the gym, this time on one of the cardio machines. A woman had just finished her cardio workout three machines away from me and went to get a paper towel sprayed with cleaner to wipe down her machine. As she made her way back, I noticed that she was heading straight for me with her eye on my water bottle which was resting in the holder attached to the handlebars of the machine. She walked right up to me, took my water bottle, threw me a look, and turned to walk away. I responded (mindfully, might I mention) by asking her why she was taking my water bottle, at which point she looked back in confusion, looked around at the other machines, saw the machine she had been using, and realized that she thought that I had taken the machine that she had been on. Her water bottle was still sitting in the holder of her machine, and when she saw it, her face turned bright red with embarrassment and she replaced my water bottle back from where she had taken it, mumbling an apology as she embarrassedly bolted away. I felt an instant surge of compassion for her, and immediately recognized the irony of the situation. I could not believe the timing, the context, and the similarities to what I had experienced just a few months earlier. I knew in that moment that life was truly making sure that the lesson I had learned with my own water bottle was being reinforced.

Learning just how wrong I can be seems to be part of the higher learning life has in store for me, a curriculum steeped in humility and acceptance. There are a few moments that come to mind in which, when faced with the reality of a situation, I have had no choice but to fess up to how misguided my version of events was and have my share of humble pie.

When I was in England one year to celebrate my birthday, my friends took me out for a celebratory dinner at a remote, country pub that doubled as a Thai restaurant. I had been there for dinner once before and had no trouble choosing somewhere I would like to eat for my birthday dinner. And let me just say that there is something so special about being in the middle of the English countryside and finding a place like this pub that had all the charms one would expect of it, while also being offered a Thai dinner experience that is so unexpected and lush that it turns the outing into an event.

We arrived and were seated, ordered our food and were brought our meals. Throughout the evening, every now and again, the ambient music playing in overhead speakers would stop abruptly, and the sounds of a turntable needle lowering onto a scratched vinyl would erupt from the sound system. At inappropriate volume, the strains of "Happy Birthday" would begin, obviously at the behest of other celebrating diners, and a procession of two or three waitresses in Thai attire would walk into the dining area, the first carrying a cake with lit candles to the celebrating table. The ambiance was just lovely, and a part of me wondered if I would get the same birthday treatment.

After we had finished our main courses and the dishes had been cleared from the table, the speakers once again fell silent and kicked back up again with the scratchy sounds of the best version of "Happy Birthday" that 1971 could offer. I felt a smile creep onto my face and looked at my friends with a look of mock horror, as if to say, "What have you done? I'm so embarrassed, am I going to be the center of attention?", all the while feeling so happy to know that my friends had thought of me. Out of the swinging door that led to the pub side of the establishment came the procession of two waitresses, a cake with lit candles held up by the one in the lead, and they headed straight towards us. I squirmed with excitement in my seat, looked from my smiling friends to the approaching waitresses and back, rolled my eyes at the retro campiness of the scene with the music playing, turned towards the procession that was making its way towards me and kept my gaze firmly glued to the cake being held aloft as it got right to me and then passed me right by as the waitresses made their way to a neighbouring table. The cake was not for me. What was for me, however, burst out of the aforementioned swinging door in the hands of another waitress who scurried over to our table and lay down a glass filled with ice cream in front of me. She looked at me and muttered under her breath, "So sorry, happy birthday", and scurried away.

I felt like my brain was short-circuiting. A part of me was still committed to that cake parade being for me while another part was recognizing just how off the mark I had been while another part was aware of my friends laughing hysterically at the scene that had just unfolded in front of them. I suspect that the picture of me sitting there with a cup of melting ice cream only added to the tragedy of what had just occurred, but I was not too proud to recognize just how funny the whole situation was and broke down in a fit of uncontrollable laughter. What added to the hilarity was not the fact that my friends had obviously taken the cheaper birthday option, it was that I am lactose intolerant and could not even eat the ice cream. I learned that evening in the remote English countryside that having my cake and eating it too was aiming much too high, that sometimes there is no cake to eat.

Another harmful pattern of thinking that has been my bedfellow for much of my life is the proclivity to catastrophize and disqualify any and all reason when anxiety takes over, especially when it comes to health-related issues. And as heavy as that might seem, that thought pattern resulted in one of the funniest and cringiest stories I have in my narrative, again taking place in England.

One year, shortly before I was leaving to spend time with friends in England, I started dating someone and felt good about the connection we seemed to have been developing. A few days after arriving in England I noticed a rash developing on the sides of my torso. My immediate thought was that I had picked up a sexually transmitted infection, and my thoughts began to spiral into near panic. All of the possible scenarios began to play out in my mind: other symptoms that might present, having the symptoms get bad enough to warrant seeking out medical help in the tiny village my friends lived in, having to tell my friends that I had potentially contracted something sexually. My mind went into overdrive and not only shifted back into the all-too familiar emotional realm of *what if*, but stayed there for the duration of a full, sleepless night. Instead of considering how I may have just been having a reaction to a different soap or something else I had been in contact with, my mind traveled down the well-trodden avenues of panic and, in that case and time, worst-case scenario.

I kept a close eye on the situation, not breathing a word of my anxiety to anyone out of shame, constantly trying to manage my emotions (which seemed even more volatile given that I was far away from the comforts of home), and upon my return, I made an appointment with my dermatologist. I mentioned in passing to my mother that I had managed to get an appointment to see the dermatologist (without telling her why I was going), which was somewhat of an accomplishment as he was extremely in demand and the waiting list to see him was normally months-long. My mom decided that she needed to also take advantage of the opportunity and asked if I minded if she came with me to the appointment so the doctor could look at an ingrown toenail that was causing her discomfort. Happy to not only get her toenail looked at, but to also have a lift to the hospital to see the doctor, I agreed to go together under the assumption that we would be called in to see the doctor separately. That did not happen.

Our dermatologist worked at a teaching hospital for medical students affiliated with one of the universities. After my mother and I were directed to a room to wait for the doctor in, the door opened and in he walked, accompanied by four or five students who were shadowing him as part of their training. He had always been a no-bullshit kind of guy, getting right to the point sometimes even before any “hi” or “how are you?” could be uttered. Without asking why we were both in the room, he brusquely asked, “Ok, so why are you here?”, to which I silently raised my shirt to expose the rash on either side of my torso.

"Ok, so what could this be?" he asked the students flanking him to either side.

"A contact dermatitis?" suggested one.

"Possibly. What else?" responded the doctor.

"An allergic reaction?" replied another student.

"Could be." Said the doctor. "What else could it be?"

total silence

The doctor looked directly at me and asked, "It could be secondary syphilis. Have you been in sexual contact with any strangers or prostitutes over the last little while?"

an eternity of total silence

crickets

tumbleweed

At this point in the conversation, parts of my mind went into panic-overdrive, a rapid succession of micro-thoughts and inner voices flying in and out of awareness. "Did I catch an infection?", "Nooooooooooooooooo!", "Should I mention it?", "Noooooooooooooooo!", "There is NO way I can say that in front of my MOTHER!", "Nooooooooooooooooo!", "Keep your mouth shut and get this appointment over with".

Using my outside voice, I mumbled that I had not had any sexual contact with anyone, including prostitutes, at which point the doctor wrote me a prescription to treat contact dermatitis and he moved onto examining my mother's toe.

In the car on the way back from the appointment, my mother asked me as we drove away, "Aren't you glad you got that checked out? What a relief!", to which I grunted something that resembled an agreement. Once out of the car and back at work, I called my family doctor who I had always had an open, honest relationship with. I eventually got the receptionist on the phone and started babbling, "I just came from the dermatologist, and I might have secondary syphilis!" She put me on hold, spoke to the doctor, came back on the line, and told me to come in immediately. I ran out of work and to the second doctor's office of the day where the receptionist and doctor were both waiting for me. I went into the examination room and lifted up my shirt to show the doctor the rash, to which he replied giggling, "That is not syphilis, put your shirt back down and use the ointment he prescribed you."

Despite knowing that the person I had met and been intimate with was most likely not to blame, despite knowing that I had not frequented any prostitutes, despite not having any other symptoms aside from the rash on the sides of my torso, the part of my mind that had spent years and years jumping to worst-case scenarios went right back there while in the UK and stayed in that mind space for the next few weeks, right up until I saw my doctor.

My mother was always vigilant when it came to illnesses, and it obviously contributed to tinges of hypochondria in my own adult life. When my brothers and I were children, our Jewish mother's faith in antibiotics seemed to rival, if not surpass, her faith in anything Judaic, and it would have been unusual to go a full year without someone taking antibiotics for some illness which, now, when seen in retrospect, possibly just needed some patience to ride out symptoms with a healthy dose of calm. I grew to learn to take her vigilance with a grain of salt to break my patterns of catastrophizing, but when she called me recently before I was leaving to go to Greece, I began to see her pattern as amusing.

I was days away from leaving for the annual wellness trip when my mother called and expressed her concern about the brush and forest fires which were ravaging the mainland there. At first, she expressed concern for my breathing, telling me the smoke might trigger my childhood asthma. I told her that I was far from the fires on the island I was going to, not to worry. She then switched tactics, asking me if I could bring swimming goggles. I told her I had my snorkel and goggle set which I was bringing along, to which she told me that I should wear the goggles as I walked around every day to spare my eyes the burn of the smoke from the fires. She wanted me to walk around, in broad daylight, in Greece, wearing swimming goggles. I. Cannot. Make. This. Up. But I digress. My mom was momming, in a very on-brand kind of way for her.

How my perception contributes to my experience of suffering, how my proclivity to focus on one part of a situation and discredit any other parts which might coexist, or how my rigid rule-keeping makes me feel like I am turning into the hard-ass, Clint Eastwood-type old guy sitting on his front porch armed with his opinions and a sawed-off shotgun, is, as it turns out, not my mother's responsibility, but mine. In doing my research and working with my own potentially harmful and unconstructive patterns of thinking, I have become all-too aware of how often cognitive distortions kick in and how they work.

We are all at the mercy of cognitive distortions which affect our thought processes and our ability to interpret, categorize, discriminate, classify, and make sense of all the information which arises within our awareness. The word "cognitive" relates back to the word *cognition*, which is often described or defined as the process of, or relating to, thinking, remembering, knowing, or perceiving. And so cognitive distortions are incorrect, unhelpful, detrimental, and potentially harmful patterns of thinking that distort reality. These cognitive distortions not only negatively alter our understanding of any given situation, but they also warp our predictive abilities. This means that because these unhelpful patterns of thinking are at work, our ability to predict potential outcomes accurately and objectively gets compromised. (See the end of this chapter for a comprehensive list of cognitive distortions).

What I think and feel to be true and the rigidity with which I adhere to it, even when I am inadequately informed or simply unwilling to be swayed, directly affects my experience of life by instigating and informing what I do and say. I know that I can fall into dichotomous, black and white, all or nothing, thinking. I can be rigid in what I believe to be acceptable and not in certain circumstances and situations. I, for instance, believe that people who steal my water bottle need to be schooled. I also believe that people who live in close proximity to one another should be mindful of the noise they make so not to disturb their neighbours, especially at certain times and on certain days of the week. I think it is reckless for cars to drive at breakneck speed down residential streets. I believe it is unacceptable for people to fart in enclosed spaces like airplanes without, at some point, getting up to go to the bathroom. And speaking of airplanes, I believe that there is a special place in hell reserved for people who sneeze and propel their sneeze into the open air in front of them. The same goes for bare feet on a plane. Same goes for pulling out a hard-boiled egg to gnaw on while on a flight. There are apparently many special places in hell.

I think it is annoying when unruly children remain unruly in public while their parents sit reading or tuning out, or even worse, allow for the behaviour by not imposing some form of structure or discipline with the child (can you tell I have no kids?). I like things a certain way. I like a certain order to the world. I consider adherence to that order to be a sign of maturity (cognitive distortion?). I also consider my proclivity towards order to be the cause of my own suffering because a) this kind of thinking is completely devoid of compassion or empathy towards the situations and realities of others, and b) that order, that stability which I would love to see around me, is virtually impossible in a world defined by impermanence, a world in which the only real constant is that everything is in a never-ending state of change and transformation.

The human brain seeks out stability within the lived experience of life, which is defined and informed by change, and so, there is dissonance, there is suffering. I want order in an existence that is defined by chaos. And in understanding this point of conflict, with the intention of doing what I can to alleviate the suffering I may be contributing to through my own rigidity, biases, and opinions, I have learned to identify in moments of suffering how my own thoughts and beliefs may be somehow distorting a situation, how my brain's need to have some sort of life preserver to hold onto may be colouring my perception in unhelpful ways.

One of my stories of actual physical suffering stems from how I invited change into my life but did it without having enough information to go on and disqualifying information that would have forced me to rethink my choice. Without doing my due diligence, I got as close to childbirth as I ever want to get.

When I was in my initial years of yoga study and teaching, I decided I was going to adopt a vegan diet, which, given the fact that I was essentially raised by The Flintstones, was a major pivot. I was, and still am, ethically aligned to the concept of doing no harm to animals and not consuming any food or products in which animals were involved. Initially, the switch felt effortless. I got a couple of vegan cookbooks, made meals which tasted incredible, and generally felt like I was doing something great for myself, animals, the earth, and my body. And then I flew to Mexico to co-lead my first yoga retreat.

As the plane was descending, I began to feel an odd burning sensation on one side of my lower back. I shrugged it off, figuring that I was dehydrated from the flight. The sensation lingered in the airport and then intensified in the hire car bringing us to the retreat centre. We had an hour drive ahead of us, and as my partner and my friend chatted and laughed, I sat in my seat quietly, convinced that my appendix was bursting and that I was going to die in Mexico. I irrationally believed that if I told them what was happening, we would need to reroute to a hospital which would put a major kink in not only the day, but the yoga retreat. So, I sat silently, waiting for my appendix to explode.

When we finally arrived at the retreat centre, I bolted out of the car, not-so-casually mentioning that I felt like I had to pee, which I did. The urge was so intense that I felt like I might pass out. I asked someone where the bathroom was, went in, and started peeing. Sort of. Because the flow was partially blocked by something. Until I felt and then actually saw something pop out into the toilet, a tiny little object I could only guess was a pebble of some sort. And in that moment, I understood that I had just passed a kidney stone.

Vegan diets are plant-based, which means that when I cut out animal products, I was eating legumes, greens, nuts, and other foods that were high in calcium oxalate. What I quickly found out was that my body was not able to process all that calcium oxalate, and just like a baby making its way through the birth canal, I birthed, through my urinary tract, a calcium oxalate baby which was tinier than a pinprick, wreaked havoc on my body, and which, for all intents and purposes, was eligible for Mexican citizenship due to its being birthed on Mexican soil. I stood staring into the toilet at my Mexican kidney stone, feeling the pain in my body begin to abate, flushed the toilet, and walked back out and filled everyone in on what had just happened. And then began to consider how what had happened could have been avoided.

I went full tilt onto that vegan diet; no slow transition, no consideration of how perhaps I needed to maintain some aspects of my normal diet due to maladaptive genes I may have had in relation to a plant-based diet, no regard for how I had been raised on a robust carnivorous diet for decades leading to my decision. I just went all-in. All-or-nothing assumptions informed the switch, and undergoing the single most painful experience of my life was the result. I decided I was going to go back to a more balanced diet which included animal products while being mindful of my consumption, which was the right thing to do for me, but which did not prevent a second kidney stone from forcing its way into the world six months later in a hospital bathroom back in my home city. That one got Canadian citizenship.

Just because my perception leads me to a conclusion does not make that conclusion true or appropriate. The first-degree-ness of deciding I would change how I nourished my body and not even considering how that might not be the wisest decision never even crossed my mind. And just because I thought my appendix was bursting did not mean that what was happening had anything to do with my appendix. What I have learned is that just because I might perceive something to be true does not necessarily make it true as an absolute, it just presents as subjectively true to me on a first-degree level, and first-degree appearances are just that, first-degree and obvious. If all we did in life was perceive and respond to life based on first-degree cues and assumptions, which we regularly do, how much truth and reality would we be missing? How much of the beauty and good stuff would we miss? What would life and humanity be like if we did not dig deeper than superficial beliefs and assumptions to find meaning, commonality, and truth? Some might say that the answer to that question could be answered by taking a cold, long look at the state of humanity today.

The opportunity to not jump to conclusions popped up again years ago when my partner was diagnosed with a cancerous lesion on his leg and the dermatologist who diagnosed it told him that it might be indicative of other cancers in the body, specifically the colon. Because the doctor did not arrange for him to be followed up by a gastroenterologist, instead leaving us both to panic and scramble to find out what the next step should be to see if there was indeed cancer in his colon, we were overcome with fear and uncertainty. Because my tendency is to fall quickly into the emotional mind instead of the logical, reasoning mind, and because that tendency goes hand in hand with catastrophizing, I went into full panic mode, observing the well-trodden pull towards jumping to worst-case scenarios, almost drowning in the fear of the *what-ifs*.

Two days before getting this call from the dermatologist, my partner had been to our family doctor for his annual checkup which included general bloodwork. After hearing the potentially devastating news from the dermatologist, I got in touch with our GP to let him know what was happening, and he replied telling me that we needed to relax, that nothing out of the ordinary had been found in the bloodwork, that if there had been a serious issue with cancerous cells, they would have shown up in the results. Because of this information, I quickly understood that my work in this situation was to balance out my fear by going into the reasoning, logical mind and reminding my heart what my head knew. Concretely speaking, we had bloodwork that somewhat disproved our fears that the colon cancer was present. And so, as my emotions got the better of me, my work was to mentally meet those emotions and thoughts with an inner dialog that dispelled their stronghold of fear over me, assuaging my fears with the facts that our family doctor had passed onto me, and extricating myself from the all too familiar cognitive distortions which previously had brought me into catastrophic thinking. It was one of my greatest lessons in not letting my emotions get the better of me and beginning to flex the muscle of meeting fear with whatever evidence I had that could disprove my worries and help dissipate my anxiety.

By understanding how unchecked perceptions do us a disservice, by understanding how the unmonitored and untethered mind works, by bringing presence of mind into any given moment, we can understand more about who and how we show up in the world, and how the meaning we assign onto everything affects our experience of life. By having some sort of practice, a reminder of how our thoughts meander down predictable and identifiable avenues, we can finally observe the mind and our thoughts as separate from us. We can mindfully observe what our perceptions are and how they may just need to be questioned, recontextualized, dismantled, and invalidated. Knowing how the mind is not always our friend and how thoughts are not always true or helpful is what we should all be remembering as we navigate life's ups and downs. After all, perception is usually changeable with added information and context, so remembering that the mind is leading us to ill-informed conclusions based on lack of evidence is usually a good tool to keep as an ongoing mindfulness practice.

ADDENDUM

Here are some of the cognitive distortions that first came to light with the work done by psychiatrist Aaron T. Beck in the early 1970's:

1) Catastrophizing: giving more weight or credence to the worst possible outcome, imagining disasters and worst-case scenarios resulting from one negative aspect of a situation. One way we catastrophize is by immediately envisioning worst-case scenarios and having them influence the decisions we make.
2) Jumping to conclusions: making a prediction or coming to a conclusion, usually negative, in the absence of any evidence that supports that prediction/conclusion. One way we jump to conclusions is by assuming we know how someone feels about us even when that assumption is not based in fact or evidence.
3) Filtering: focusing on the negative aspects of a situation while excluding the positive or filtering out information that does not support current beliefs or opinions. One way we

filter is when we get both positive and negative feedback, but only focus on the negative. If 10 people are in attendance when you give a presentation and nine of them love what you presented, but one person did not, you would filter out the nine and focus on the one.

4) Overgeneralizing: coming to a conclusion with little or only one piece of evidence instead of getting all the information necessary to properly formulate that conclusion. One way we overgeneralize is by assuming that the way events and situations unfolded in the past dictates how similar events and situations will unfold in the future.

5) Emotional reasoning: basing one's opinion entirely on whatever feelings or emotions are present. One way we reason emotionally is by believing that whatever fears we may have in relation to a situation are indicative of a reason to fear, are valid, and that no other possibilities exist. Just because we feel a certain way about something does not necessarily make it true.

6) Labelling: defining our character or the character of others based on actions exhibited in specific situations that do not represent the entirety of who we, or they, are. One way we label ourselves is when we call ourselves stupid because we messed up a job interview instead of feeling compassion for having been affected by stress. This cognitive distortion can also be referred to as *mislabeling*.

7) Rigidity: seeing life in a black and white way, with no grey areas. Rigidity is adhering to rules, laws, and ways of operating with little tolerance for other approaches or opinions. One way we can be rigid is by thinking that there is only one way to go about a certain activity, and if we or someone else goes about it another way, we feel instability, anger, or impatience.

8) Blowing things out of proportion: when the response is not in proportion to the activating event. Making a massive deal out of something that was not intended to offend or hurt. One way this can occur is when we show up at a scheduled time to meet a friend, but that friend ends up being late due to traffic, and we get angry at them for making us wait. The holdup was beyond their control, and to get angry over an unavoidable delay is making a mountain out of a molehill.

Other cognitive distortions exist which expound on the ones mentioned here, but for the sake of introducing these patterns, the ones mentioned above will suffice.

PUT THE NEEDLE ON THE RECORD

At the turn of the twenty-first century, I was a year or two into my yoga practice. I was living on a street right next to Parc Lafontaine in Montreal, nearing the end of a nine-year relationship that I had held onto desperately because I knew that when it ended, I was going to be faced with me, myself, and I, and I was a bundle of insecurity and uncertainty. My relationship was not doing well for many reasons, the most glaring of all being that I had no idea who I was. I had no sense of self or Self. Enter yoga. For some reason, yoga was somehow on my radar at the time, and so I decided to research it and see if it was something I wanted to learn more about.

I remember going to Mélange Magique, a store commonly referred to as "the witchcraft store", but which sold more than Wiccan literature and accessories. The place was great. They sold books on religions and philosophies, sacred traditions, and rituals. They also had books on yoga and Hinduism, and I would hang out there browsing, reading, and feeling oddly comfortable in what theoretically should have been a strange environment.

After perusing most, if not all, of the yoga-related books and references, I eventually bought a box of yoga flash cards. Flash cards are like a deck of playing cards, and this deck's cards each had a different posture on it, colour coded depending on the type of posture it displayed (seated, standing, forward bend, backbend, etc.). I remember bringing the set home and sitting on the green industrial carpet of my then-bedroom. I laid the cards out and started to build my own home practice that I kept going a few times a week.

After practicing alone for a few months, I decided I needed to start looking for a proper yoga teacher. The door number of my address at that time was 964. After doing some digging, I found a teacher, one who just so happened to live directly across the street from me. Joan Ruvinsky's door number was 987. I registered for a yoga session along with a couple of friends, and all I really remember is that after the second class I got up from my yoga carpet and felt like I had just ingested something magical. I felt relaxed and alive and peaceful and happy. I felt high without having consumed any drugs. And so, I kept at it, registering for session after session.

The years that succeeded that first session were heavy for me. My relationship did indeed end, my grandmother passed away, a friend died in the Twin Towers on September 11, 2001, and one of my dogs died. Every time something happened, I'd phone Joan and leave her a message to let her know that I wouldn't be finishing the current session that I'd been registered for, as I was so beaten up emotionally that I couldn't commit to showing up for classes. And it was in 2001 when I called her, post 9/11, that I got her on the phone and, after hearing my reasoning for not finishing the session, she gently said to me, "Consider the possibility that times like these are when you most need the practice." What a teaching moment that was. She changed my life with that one line.

Around the same time, I decided to book a private coaching session with her. I needed to talk to someone about all the suffering I was experiencing, and she made time for me. We went to the downstairs apartment in her greystone, terraced townhouse, sat on comfortable chairs, the room lit by the soft glow of the lamps next to us, and I talked and talked. When I was done, she looked at me and matter-of-factly said, "Bram, you just have to get out of your own way." I nodded, doing my best to appear as if I understood what she was saying, made some sounds which I hoped conveyed that she was definitely giving me something to think about, and we wound up the session. I remember crossing the street on my way home thinking, "What the hell did she mean by '*get out of your own way*'?" and chalked my confusion up to not being smart enough to understand the meaning of the phrase.

I continued taking classes with Joan, often veering away from the practice, and then coming back, over and over throughout the years, which seems to be the path for so many people when it comes to their wellness practices. It was a few years later, when I was studying yoga scriptures intensively on my own, that I finally understood what Joan was trying to tell me. By telling me to get out of my own way, Joan was telling me that the meaning I was assigning onto all the events that I had felt were debilitating enough to warrant stopping what brought me joy, such as the yoga practice, was mine and mine alone to assign. I, albeit unconsciously, had assigned meaning to the ending of my relationship and the bodily deaths of my loved ones. That meaning I had assigned was that these were the most horrible things that a human being could live through and bear witness to, and that life was a horribly unfair and cruel journey. Full stop. No wonder I was having so much difficulty simply existing. The weight of all these horrible events was crushing the joy out of me. And then came Joan's words.

"You just have to get out of your own way". Joan had subtly introduced the concept of Patanjali's yoga sutra that tells us to think of opposite thoughts in the presence of negative ones, to recontextualize the situation that is bringing suffering. We learn by this wisdom that by cultivating positive or helpful thoughts, we experience what is deemed positive as a felt-sense experience, which often includes ease, comfort, peace, contentment, and relaxation. By cultivating positive thoughts, we cultivate positive emotions, and by cultivating positive emotions, we move closer to the experiences of resilience, clarity, wellness, and health. In applying this teaching and passing it onto me, Joan was in no way trying to trick me into thinking that the challenging circumstances I was experiencing were not indeed happening. She was just gently reminding me that in the presence of what is deemed negative, in the presence of adversity and that which makes me uncomfortable, there are other perspectives available to reframe the situations and assign new meaning to them. By telling me to get out of my own way, Joan was sparking the understanding that if I interpreted whatever was going on as debilitating, then it would be exactly that. She was telling me that the events would carry whatever meaning I assigned to them. And so, in order to get out of my own way, in order to empower myself instead of disempowering myself, I could reframe the situations to see how they were teaching me instead of hobbling me. I could see how they were markers on my spiritual journey of growth and understanding instead of simply being what left me feeling hopeless, helpless, and alone.

Not only was this wisdom a massive revelation for me, but it also proved to be forever empowering in its quiet simplicity, a simplicity that taught me that I had a choice as to how I responded to events occurring that previously would have left me grieving and incapacitated. The death of a loved one became the bodily death of a loved one, not an absolute full stop. Events not unfolding in a hoped-for or anticipated manner became life allowing me to dodge a bullet, understanding that if events had unfolded in an anticipated way, I would perhaps have been somehow worse off due to some unforeseen twist of fate. A relationship not working out became a marker to keep moving forwards, perhaps to another one that would be healthier. Catching a cold became an opportunity to neutrally observe illness run its course as part of the changing landscape I could bear witness to. One more event in the endless stream of events, all of which could be neutrally observed and responded to instead of being metaphorical threats to my contentment that held my attention, emotions and breathing hostage. Joan changed my entire life with that one piece of wisdom-steeped advice, and she allowed me to figure out what it meant on my own instead of telling me and projecting her meaning onto it. She allowed me to create my own meaning from the wisdom of a few words written down millennia ago, wisdom that not only informs Hinduism and yoga philosophy but is also at the root of psychotherapeutic tools that have helped countless people finally make sense of what previously had been incomprehensible. Changing response tactics: that is what Joan taught me. How to change response tactics because, as it turns out, the wise advice telling us that if we want a different outcome, we need to do something differently is actually true. It seems so obvious and simple, and yet to do something differently, to respond wisely instead of reacting to life not going as planned, can sometimes feel near impossible.

I have a family member who, whenever life deals a harsh blow, becomes lost in the grief and sadness of things not going as planned (which he expresses as anger and disappointment), of once again being knocked down when he hoped that, finally, he might get what he truly wants out of life. I have had many a conversation with him in these moments, conversations in which I need to balance out my desire to steer him in a productive way with the knowledge that he might only want a shoulder to cry on, not someone telling him what to do. Because I am so familiar with his pattern of falling into despair and feeling sorry for himself and his lot in life, I made it a priority to find the words and wisdom I could in order to accompany him responsibly while also guiding him out of his well-traveled patterns of torment. In doing so, I realized that the fundamental difference between him and myself is that when life does not go according to my best-laid plans, I do not tend to throw a pity party. I instead kick into persistence/rebel-mode, either getting galvanized to not give up and keep trying until I get what I set out to achieve or to have somewhat of a *"this obviously is not for me"* attitude about whatever the situation is, allowing me to let it go completely and set my sights on something else I can direct my energy towards and put value and importance on.

When I was single and dating, I remember feeling hopelessly despondent when relationships were not working out. One person after another, I found myself once again single and sitting at home alone, wailing at the tragedy of having so much love to give but no one to give it to. And then, one day, as if a light switch had been turned on in my brain, I concluded that I was no longer going to grieve for what did not work out but was going to adopt the "Prochain / Next" attitude. "Prochain (French for "next") / Next" is sometimes what is heard from cashiers in shops and supermarkets in Montreal when they are done ringing up one client's transaction and want to call the next client to the register. The expression insinuates a methodical, non-emotional approach to efficiently getting on with it, and so I decided I was going to approach dating as if I were at the cash register passing transaction after transaction, confident that at a certain point, someone who I wanted to stick around would show up at the register looking for more than a simple transaction. I rebelled against getting crushed at every letdown and decided to attack the process of meeting the right person with a vengeance that had no room for feeling sorry for myself. And this new way of thinking, this rejection of getting pulled back into that old default of pity and self-flagellation, proved to be massively successful after only a few months, allowing me to find a relationship I believed was waiting for me.

I decided to tell my family member that perhaps letting go of his default pity-party and adopting an attitude that was closer to "don't-give-up-until-you-get-what-you-want" might prove to be the missing link in his equation. Initially, he met me with resistance, telling me that he had already done that over and over and it had amounted to nothing, telling me that he was so tired of trying, telling me that this was obviously his lot in life and that life sucked and was unfair. I did not push it. I gave him a hug and we moved onto different conversations. A week later he texted me to let me know that he had decided that he was going to try this new avenue, seeing every letdown as a pointer directing him away from feeling sorry about himself and towards trying even harder, recommitting to whatever he wanted out of a situation. And the change in him is, to this day, magnificent. He has changed. He has become more confident. He has morphed into this person who only takes no for an answer when it really is the only answer, but he does all the due diligence necessary before getting there.

I have operated in specific ways for the entirety of my life. I have been navigating specific neural pathways in the brain, processing information, reacting, speaking, and showing up in my life in extremely specific ways. Essentially, I have been using specific brain channels in my patterns of thinking and doing, channels that I have revisited over and over again, avenues that I have travelled down in repetitive, mostly unconscious ways for decades. The metaphor I often use to help others understand this concept involves vinyl records. If you consider that your brain is like a vinyl record that will have grooves pressed into it as soon as it is used, then the second you begin to use the thinking mind, as soon as you begin to speak and act according to the conclusions you have come to and the customs and rituals you have been taught, then you begin to lower the needle onto the record, not to land inside a pre-cut groove, but to create the groove itself. When you begin to think in patterns, the needle begins to carve out, to deepen, the existing grooves that represent your thought patterns. And as you age, you continually revisit these same grooves, these same thought patterns and processes that inevitably result in the same behaviours, actions, and reactions.

When Joan suggested I get out of my own way, she was suggesting that I lift the needle out of the pre-worn grooves, the ones I had exhausted over and over until I was miserable, and intentionally lower the needle onto a new section of the vinyl that had not been used before. To change one's thought patterns and approach to any situation or context is to create new grooves, ones in which more helpful avenues of analysis and thought are created, which can only result in different outcomes, different epiphanies, different modes of response and states of being. Getting out of my own way meant creating new grooves in the vinyl of my mind, using different brain channels to interpret and disseminate information, so that the same old result of unhappiness could be replaced by another, ideally opposite, state, a practice I mastered at the dentist's office, of all places.

Years ago, I was lying in the chair at the dentist's office with my mouth wired open, some sort of balloon-type stretchy material attached to the wires, feeling very claustrophobic while also feeling like some sort of horror film character. I was there to get a couple of fillings replaced, and just sitting there with my jaw wired open, breathing through my mouth like some sort of swamp monster, brought back my childhood terror of going to the dentist.

When I was a kid the combination of the clinical smell of the dentist's office and having his stubby fingers and metal instruments clanging around in my mouth always made my body tense up. It became so intense that the second I saw him advancing to take a look inside my mouth, I would gag. Going to the dentist's office became traumatic and stayed that way. Throughout the years I gradually got better at dealing with it, learning to breathe through my nose deeply to get through it, but I never could shake the way my body would freeze up when I had to lie there getting my teeth and gums cleaned.

Cut to a few years ago with my mouth wired open horror-film style. I am breathing slowly and deeply, working to maintain calm even though I am petrified as the dentist approaches my mouth with a needle to anesthetize the area he would be working in. I keep breathing, he injects the needle, I taste that acrid taste of the anesthetic, and we wait a minute or two for it to kick in. It doesn't. He injects another needle with more anesthetic. No luck. Another. Same. Five more needles, one after the other, until I finally cannot feel any sensation where he needs to do his work and suspect that I am now drooling like the swamp monster I believe I have turned into.

As this butchery is taking place, I realize that my forearms are contracted, and my hands are balled up into fists. I may be breathing slowly and deeply but my body has tensed up again as it has every time I have been in the dentist's chair since childhood. Instead of staying in that state of muscular lockdown as I have repeatedly in the past, I decide I am going to do something differently. I decide to identify what I am feeling. Hot, searing, localized pain in my mouth. I then decide I am going to identify the opposite of these sensations. Cool, non-localized ease and openness. I begin to scan my body to see if I can locate an area that is not locked down with tension, an area in which I can find cool, non-localized ease and openness. And I do, in my forearms, which begin to release and ease up, the sensations of coolness and relaxation replacing the rigidity and tautness, and I intentionally focus on that. My mind oscillates from the pain in my mouth to the ease in my arms, back and forth, like I am watching a tennis match. But I eventually spend more time focused on my forearms and feel the rest of my body relaxing. It was revelatory. I realize that I am responding to physical and emotional discomfort differently, in a way that is replacing terror with calm and peace at the dentist's office, the site of my past terror. This concept is at the heart of Hindu and yogic philosophy, as it is with cognitive-based psychotherapeutic tools like reframing and CBT (Cognitive Behavioural Therapy). Change your thought, change your mind, change the meaning you assign, change the action you take, change the outcome, change the fallout, change your world. It was a true epiphany, one that had me feeling like I was overcoming some major hurdles and the hold that they had had on me for so many years.

I got out of my own way at the dentist's office, and getting out of my own way continues to be a lifelong mindfulness practice. Don't get me wrong, this process did not happen for me all at once, and it most likely will not for you. However, like any muscle we want to build, it involves using it again and again, over and over, until what previously had been the result of intentional effort becomes more of a second-nature, unconscious response. All that was needed for me was awareness of how discomfort shifted me into harmful patterns of thinking and, subsequently, action, and continuously altering that trajectory until it became less of an effort and more of a wise default response. This kind of wisdom is available to every single one of us and will inevitably result in a much more enjoyable lived experience.

Every single one of us is capable of finding new ways, exploring new avenues, creating new grooves in the record of our mind, because isn't that what life is? Isn't life the opportunity to move closer to truth and wisdom with every day we are above ground? Isn't life the ability to learn from the higher learning life has in store for each of us and move onwards and upwards with the new lessons we extrapolate from the drama, the fear, the uncertainty, and the instability? When we change the groove in which the needle is doing its thing, we are choosing to test life, to see if it is actually possible to experience life in a different way by choosing to put our faith in new ways, new hopes and beliefs. With every small step in a new direction, we find ourselves moving towards epiphanies and realizations that point back to how we have, essentially, limited ourselves and what we have believed to be possible based purely in the habits and patterns we had been adhering to for far too long.

CHANGEABLE

"Though I lack the art
to decipher it,
no doubt the next chapter
in my book of transformations
is already written.
I am not done with my changes."

– Excerpt from *The Layers* by Stanley Kunitz

I know that I am meant to accompany people throughout life in many iterations. I know that through the modalities of writing, teaching, lecturing, podcasting, giving wellness trips around the world, and coaching, I am meant to be a source of trust and support, of accompaniment. That knowledge, however, only became evident to me after decades of feeling lost and unsure of what to do with my life. In my mid-thirties and at the end of a successful career in managing stores for an American retailer, I decided I was going to pay attention to the knowings which were whispering to me. I had grown sick of selling disposable crap to people who did not need it and knew on a visceral level that I wanted to help people heal. When I went for dinner with a friend and shared my fear at knowing that I was leaving a career that offered stability and a sense of safety to jump into the unknown, she innocently asked me what I would do with my time if money, geography, and education were not factors. I immediately answered that I would teach yoga and write. And she just looked at me. And then she shrugged as if to say, "So what's stopping you?"

That shrug was the catalyst for a cataclysmic life change. I knew that from that moment on there was no going back, that there was no plan b, that I was now on a course whose destination was unknown, and that no matter what, my life would be different going forwards. As someone who knew how fear could hold me back from taking chances, I recognized that I was breaking old patterns of fear-based inaction so that I could rebuild my life in wholeness, blurring the lines between work and passion. The rest, as they say, is history.

I believe that people can change their habits and ways of thinking. Every one of us can change. We can break through old patterns of rigidity and fear, we can move through the paralysis that intense emotions can elicit, we can refuse to allow what we believe we lack to continue to dictate what daily life is like. The changes that I have experienced and where they have brought me in life have shown me that the true heights we dream of attaining lie on the other side of what holds us back, namely fear, grief, rigidity, and scarcity-based thinking. My experiences have shown me that life will provide opportunities to respond differently to the situations and people that trigger old patterns of defense and survival, and it is in these situations that the true life lessons await.

I believe that the first lesson I was taught in life's curriculum for me occurred when I was seven or eight years old. I was at home after school watching *Three's Company*, a show about a heterosexual guy who wanted to move into an apartment with two heterosexual women but who needed to pretend to the apartment complex's owners that he was homosexual in order to be allowed to live with them. I had been watching the show for a while mindlessly, escapist television to tune into so I could tune out of life, but that afternoon I had a realization. Watching the straight guy who was pretending to be gay act the fool in front of those he was trying to deceive, and seeing those he was trying to deceive make off-the-cuff, derogatory comments about his homosexuality, hit me like a ton of bricks. I realized that I was that guy, I was the one who the world would ridicule when they found out I was gay. The farcical object of mockery was me and I was it and I felt so weighed down by the shame and embarrassment of it that I decided I was going to speak to my mother about it.

I do not remember what came after watching the show, whether it was taking a bath and then dinner or vice versa, but I remember being in the bathtub feeling the weight of the decision I had made to bare my soul to my mom and decided to just rip off the band aid. I went to the kitchen where she was and told her that I had a "problem". She sat down and asked me what my problem was, and I told her that I liked boys. With the limited amount of awareness and vocabulary I had at that time, it was the best I could do. She stared me dead in the eyes and told me that I could let go of the problem, it was no longer a problem, that she was taking it from me and that everything was going to be ok. And I felt like I could finally breathe. I felt like a massive weight had been lifted from my chest and that life was going to be ok. I had lived up to that point feeling doomed by my secret, and that moment with my mom was the turning point.

The following day, after getting home from school, my mother called me back into the kitchen where she sat me down and told me that she had gone to the library to do some research and that it was absolutely normal for boys of my age to want to be with other boys of my age. And in that moment, I felt my life stop. I felt the weight that had been lifted the previous day settle right back in like an anvil on my chest. I knew at that moment that for whatever reason, my mother had not heard me. She could not hear me. I immediately and silently assumed blame for not coming out with the words, "I am gay", words that could not have been misinterpreted, and mumbled some sort of response to her before walking away from the kitchen certain that the rest of my life was hopeless.

I now know that I walked out of the kitchen that afternoon and into the rest of my childhood as a parentified child, a child who needed to step up as the leader in his own life because his parent could not. I had stuck my neck out, bared my soul, asking to be reassured that I was ok and that I would be ok, and was essentially shot down. I am compelled to say that something broke inside of me that day, but I actually believe that the opposite is true. I believe that something was born after that incident, a part of me that kicked in and took over. This part was relegated to the fact that I was, essentially, on my own, that I could not ask for help, that I could not be, and would never be able to be, authentically myself, that I could not trust or lean on anyone but me. A strength was born that day, one that kept me functional and capable of keeping up appearances, one that saved me from whatever the other options were. That day also reinforced what

I had wanted to rid myself of, which was living in concealment. Instead of being able to free myself, however, of the constant work keeping secrets required, I resigned myself, with an incredible chasm of melancholy, to accepting that concealment would be my lifelong companion. I accepted that keeping secrets had to be my "normal" and that there would always be a duality in life, a "me" others could see and one which only I had access to.

The patterns of concealment and secrets followed me throughout the next few decades, even after I properly stood in my power and told my closest friends and family that I was gay. I still kept my cards close to my chest because that was what I had been trained by life to do. I had been conditioned to believe that if I was honest in my authenticity and true self, I would be rejected and abandoned. If I made myself as vulnerable as I had that day after watching *Three's Company*, I would be hurt a million times more intensely than I would be if I kept my cards close to my chest, so why the hell should I ever try again?

Roughly fifteen years following my unsuccessful attempt to unburden myself with my mother, she invited me to come with her for a short trip to Florida, just me and her. I had come out of the closet by then, was dating someone and was generally living my life with more honesty. I remember my mother asking me to go for a walk with her along the boardwalk near to where we were staying. As we walked side by side amongst the others on the boardwalk, she asked me how I knew if someone was gay, if there was some sort of way to identify a stranger. In hindsight, she was asking me if gaydar was actually a thing, but with all kidding aside, I knew in that moment that she was trying. She was trying to get a peek into my world, into my private logic. And in doing so, she was telling me without using the actual words that she was there for me, as much as she could be considering she was dealing with a situation and aspect of life that she not only knew absolutely nothing about, but which, I believe, scared the hell out of her. I remember getting into that conversation with her, deciding quickly to meet her where she was instead of judging her inability to meet me where I would have loved her to. And I remember feeling some sort of melancholic satisfaction with that chat we had. It was progress. Perhaps not the kind I had been dying for all those years ago when I needed her to help me feel like I was not doomed, but progress, nonetheless. Better late than never, I supposed.

Even after that conversation, and after years of therapy and over a decade into a true adult relationship, I realized that I had been living for far too long on lies and withholding. Concealment had become so deeply ingrained in me, so normalized that I had never questioned why it might actually be harmful. I had never considered that this childhood defense mechanism might not only be obsolete in my adulthood, but actually harmful to establishing and maintaining meaningful connections. And so, in my forties, I began to test the waters of standing in my integrity and doing what scared me most: being honest about everything. Yes, there was resistance from some people who could not handle whatever my truth was, and yes, that resistance triggered the old patterns of withholding in order to avoid dealing with emotional fallout. But instead of avoidance, I used my words. I let that kid who had just seen the gay character of a show be ridiculed for who he was and who thought that he was doomed speak *his* truth and stand by it. And slowly but surely, that kid got bolder, more confident, more secure, more unafraid, and began to change his approach to living in the world. I grew out of my childhood conditioning in my forties through intentional, mindful communication and a refusal to edit my inside voice as it became my outside voice. And hear me when I say that if I could do it, anyone could, regardless of whatever wounds they carry with them. Real, sustainable change can occur. Learning this for myself has been the motivating force in accompanying others through their own suffering and resistance.

Seen through a spiritual lens, I believe that life will always give us what we need as part of our higher learning through the challenges and experiences we encounter. Consider that we need to know certain things, things about ourselves as well as about life. And consider that we do not already know everything, regardless of age and experience. Change serves as the gateway to knowing what was previously unknown, the gateway to learning by gleaning what the lessons are in any given situation. We are all living the experience of getting a higher education, a life education that we were enrolled in at birth and which may kick in early in life, as mine did. All experiences contain lessons, and what matters is how we perceive the challenges we face, what we do with them, and how we assign meaning to them. With this approach, we can gravitate more easily towards working through the old patterns of resistance that life had trained us to believe were essential and believe in the possibility of things working out in our favour. I have learned through my own journey of being changeable that we do not learn when life is good, when events unfold smoothly. We learn when things are tough, when we are faced with difficulty and adversity, when emotional overwhelm seems inevitable and insurmountable. It is in those moments that we can recognize life's pitfalls and challenges as opportunities to experience a form of purification by fire, a rite of passage through which we discover who we are when faced with suffering. In the face of suffering, we either cower in fear or finally turn toward it boldly and say,

"Bring it on, let's do this." It is those moments of agency when we reclaim our power, when we decide that we will no longer spend our time feeling victimized. That is when we tap into the depths of wisdom and bravery which we all have access to. I believe this is why life's harder moments exist: to teach us, to equip us, to remind us that even if the path ahead looks endless and murky and obstructed, every one of us can stand in our power, solid and certain in our right to exist and to thrive. We just need to be mindful of staying the course, riding the process out and remembering that through mindful persistence and staying true to ourselves, we are constantly creating new, more functional and sustainable grooves in the record of who and how we are. We are changing how we interact with our thoughts, our selves and life. And, from what I have gleaned from my own experience, it is only through this process that we can discover the lifelong path of purpose and fulfillment that we all yearn for.

THE PARENTIFICATION PATH

Way back in 2004 I was asked by my close friend in England to be her newborn son's godfather, an ask that I was so honoured to say yes to. I jumped at it and quickly booked my flights to make the trip over for the christening.

At that time, I was working in retail management for a big-box, international retailer and before heading to England, I figured I would bring something along with me from the store that would make my friends laugh. The Jesus Action Figure was a hard plastic figurine of Jesus in his white robes, posable arms extended alongside his body with his palms facing upwards, affixed to a hard, cardboard backing on which images of Bethlehem were printed. What made this potentially inappropriate offering even funnier was that under his feet were wheels to give the illusion of "sliding action", as indicated on the packaging. Knowing my friends and how similar our senses of humour were, I knew I was bringing a gift that would keep us laughing for decades.

Once arrived in England, my friends absolutely loved the gift, insisting on keeping it in the packaging so the Bethlehem background could continue to give context. They immediately hung it on the kitchen wall where everyone could see it, giving everyone a laugh who came over in the days leading up to the christening. Until they knew that the village vicar was coming over for the pre-christening interview.

The day before the big visit, I was pulled aside and told by my friends that the vicar would be popping over for a chat, that it was standard practice in the Anglican church, and that not only would Jesus have to come down for the duration of the visit, but that I would have to go up. And by that, my friends meant that I needed to go upstairs and keep quiet while the vicar got all the details about the ceremony. When I inquired as to why I could not be present for the vicar's visit, seeing as how I had come all the way from Canada, I was told that my being present might pose an obstacle to godfather-certification, as my last name was Jew-ish, but with me in the room, my semitic appearance might remove the -ish and disqualify me from becoming a godfather in the Church of England.

I remember the moment as clear as day: with a healthy amount of incredulity (mixed with a dash of my oft-inappropriate sense of humour), I replied to my friends that being banished to the upper quarters of the house felt a bit too evocative of Anne Frank, but then doubled down on that line of defense when I felt I had breached the line of inappropriateness. Despite my best efforts, my mother's sick sense of humour does occasionally force its way out of my mouth. And so, the following day when the vicar appeared at the house, I scurried upstairs and stayed as quiet as a statue as the Christians handled their business downstairs in the kitchen with the Jesus Action Figure tucked away clandestinely in the crockery cabinet.

The following day, dressed in all our finery, we walked over to the village church for the christening. The ceremony began seated in pews with the vicar leading us in song to three pre-chosen hymns. And when I I realized I was the only person in that church who was unfamiliar with those songs of praise, something kicked into gear. I acted as if I was the church choirmaster. Maintaining a healthy rhythm of being one heartbeat behind everyone else with voices raised in song, I belted out telling it from the mountain, sang something about a flock and I am pretty sure there was also a verse or two devoted to giving God my heart. I sang with gusto, committed wholeheartedly to becoming this kid's godfather come hell or high water. And while many (even some reading these words) might take issue with this act of religious concealment, let me just say that I had absolved myself of religion long before that day, stoic in my refusal to participate in any faith or belief system that endorsed division and separation. And if I was going to be damned to eternal hellfire for withholding the Judaic culture I had been born into, that was a curse I was ready to assume, as long as I could go down in the annals of history as godfather to my friend's firstborn.

When it was time to stand around the baptismal font and speak with the vicar, I showed up like a champ. The conversation went like this:

Vicar: "Are you, Bram Levinson, the chosen person to be godfather to this child?"

Me: "Yes."

Vicar: "Do you turn away from Satan?"

Me, trying desperately to mask the horror of being asked that question when no one had prepared me for anything of its ilk:

"Sure."

Vicar: "Do you turn to Jesus?"

Me, feeling more comfortable discussing Jesus than the aforementioned fallen angel, "Sure."

The vicar continued with the proceedings until it came time to dab the holy water on the forehead of my soon-to-be godson and then the deed was done. It was official. We returned to the house for a celebratory meal and I breathed a much-needed sigh of relief after the whole ordeal.

There are two patterns that run throughout this story that are very indicative of how I operate in the world, which is to either fake it until I make it or jump at an opportunity without knowing what it will entail, knowing that I will figure it out. Both patterns fit into the pathology of someone who was a parentified child in their youth. Remember the story of me trying to come out to my mother when I was seven or eight years old and her not being able to hear or support me in the ways I needed? The process of realizing I was on my own to manage my thoughts and emotions, knowing that despite having put what felt like my life on the line to speak my truth I was without help in my situation, created what is referred to as "parentification".

Parentification occurs when the needs of a child are not met for whatever reason or context and the child is left to understand that they will need to take the helm of controlling their destiny. Another way of explaining parentification is by saying that when leadership in the family system is abdicated by a parent not leaving the child feeling properly parented, the child assumes leadership, potentially before they are cognitively, physically or emotionally developed and qualified to do so. I believe that I became parentified when I realized I had to deal with my sexuality on my own, that no one could help me. And what that created was a sense of self-reliance that was not chosen, but which was absolutely a survival mechanism which allowed me to not explode in a shame-filled puff of smoke that evening in the kitchen with my mother.

Much like the line, "I can make it alone" from Madonna's song Jump, taken from the 2005 *Confessions on a Dance Floor* album, I had been trained from early on to figure it out myself. And figure it out, I have, going all the way back to my school days. High school was spent walking the fine line between getting excellent grades and writing myself notes signed from my "parents" getting me out of school so I could go downtown and watch movies. My brief foray into post-secondary collegiate studies ended when I was writing the exam for one of the two courses I actually cared about. The Religious Cults and Sects course awakened my passion for spirituality when I spent the day at the Hare Krishna temple and saw what devotion looked like, but the Psychology course I had just begun was awakening my deeper need to understand the meanderings of the mind, and I was fully hooked. The Psychology exam had just begun, we were in the first semester of the course, and as I began writing, my pencil broke. Despite knowing that the teacher, a woman whose severity far surpassed the austere education I had received in the private high school I had attended, had prohibited speaking during the exam, I needed to do something about my broken pencil. I needed something to write with. I whispered to my friend sitting next to me, asking if she had an extra pencil, at which point the teacher barked at us that we had both failed the exam and that we could leave the room. I was gutted. And furious. And because I had grown accustomed to being disappointed by adults and a system that did not seem to have room for me, I threw a metaphorical middle finger up to the entire educational system and walked out the doors, intent on making my life happen my way, on my terms. Parentified, to say the least.

After years working in retail management, I decided that I wanted to study yoga and chose a training program which would provide the most comprehensive education while also immersing me in the most gruelling style and practice. Now while I was always a gymnastic type of person, flexibility was not my main attribute, so when I enrolled in an Ashtanga Yoga training, I knew I had my work cut out for me. Ashtanga seemed to be the bigger, more rigid and unforgiving brother to the vinyasa style I had adopted six months before the training started, and the others in the training were light years ahead of me in terms of ability. My dread increased on the first training weekend when the teacher, an internationally renowned Ashtanga master, told us that the practice we were immersing ourselves in was not a healing one, that any injuries we had previously healed from would be reawakened by the practice. He then showed us how he had no knee joints by raising one bent leg off the ground and showing us how his lower leg could spin in a hanging-rotating kind of way. I was petrified, but I also knew that I had committed to myself that I would finish the program because there was no plan B, I would become a certified teacher if it killed me. And when the physical practice did hurt me, when something in my back pinched during one of the daily practices, I lay down on my mat and stayed there as everyone around me finished their practices. Even then, as the odd one out lying down on my mat when I should have been honing each posture to perfect my practice, I kept going, much like I did in that tiny, quaint village church a few years earlier in England. I did it my way, quite simply because I was trained by life to keep going, to persevere in whatever ways felt intuitive, to figure it out.

There is still occasional resentment which arises within my awareness related to feeling like I have to always figure it out on my own, regardless of what "it" is. I suppose that incident with my mother shaped my expectations surrounding feeling supported and cared for, and while it would be all too easy to let myself wallow in resentment, I choose to instead understand that the world was different back then when I tried to express my truth. Resources for my mother, and access to those resources, were few and far between, and I know that not getting the relief or support I was praying for actually served me in ways that I am still uncovering to this day. That moment taught me that I would have to choose my own path, it would not be made available to me as easily as it would for others. As I grew older, I realized that choosing my own path would take the form of having to choose my own curriculums, not depending on conventional schooling to prepare me for life. Choosing what felt right instead of succumbing to what everybody else seemed to be doing absolutely sucked, but the rewards that were waiting for me, the revelations associated to feeling true freedom, have been greater than anyone could have prepared me for. Teaching myself by just doing it became my modus operandi: podcasting, giving wellness trips around the world, teaching what felt relevant to me and speaking in front of hundreds, sometimes thousands, of people, writing books. The path of a parentified child could be a path of loneliness and isolation unless one thrives on aloneness, in which case the path becomes ones of muchness and innovation.

Aside from learning from Madonna that I can make it alone, she has taught me that one needs to have deep knowledge of structure before one can break away from it, which is why I stuck it out during that year of Ashtanga Yoga training. And I got the best education I could get, learning both about what I wanted to adopt into my own methods of teaching as much as what I preferred to reject. It taught me that learning what not to do is as important, if not more, than adopting nuggets of wisdom that ring true. It taught me to continue along this path of authenticity, of doing it my own way, to forge my own, albeit parentified, path. I suspect it is because of that approach that I experience whatever success presents itself in my life and career but trust me when I say that there are moments when I would love to be ignorant. There are periods of the Bram-ness when ignorance would be, as they say, blissful, moments in which I fantasize about being that dumb, unaware person who floats through life always getting what they want, oblivious to suffering and adversity. But then again, that path of the innocent, ignorant, deer-in-the-headlights most likely would not bring me a fraction of the contentment and satisfaction that my achievements have brought me, mainly because I know I have earned it. Every second of self-reliance, every moment of jumping beyond fear-based cynicism while simultaneously yearning for mentors has taught me to do it myself. To trust that I can figure it out. To trust that this is the path I am meant to journey along, one which contains bespoke lessons and adversity meant to bring me closer to the future versions of myself that are waiting for me to get to them. And that, I believe, is practically unteachable unless the school of hard knocks knocks hard. I am so grateful for the knocks.

The path of healing, from feeling left to my own devices as a child to feeling connected to a network of support as an adult, has taught me to ask for help, to jump beyond the private logic that was created in my childhood which convinced me no one would be there for me and I would have to rely solely on me, myself and I. As I wrote in my first book, *The Examined Life*, I have learned through years of keeping my cards close to my chest that if I do not ask for help, for accompaniment, from the people who I am closest to in my life, I am treating those inner-circle people as if they were perfect strangers. Despite having been taught by life that I needed to practice concealment during the most formative of years, the path of healing through spiritual study and intense therapy has shown me that none of us really get anywhere alone. Like it or not, we need each other, we need accompaniment. And what that has taught me is that even if those I invite into the inner circle give me all the support and sympathetic ears available, at the end of it all this is the story of Bram, and what I feel is waiting for me in that story must be attained and accomplished on my own, yet with support and guidance which is requested, asked for, solicited. Deprogramming parentification has taught me to ask for help, for time, for energy from my people, but does not change the fact that, as my Mama Lil told me all those years ago when all I wanted was a Billy Idol cassette, "No one is going to do it for you." I can ask for the supporting tools and illumination along the path, but that path must be traversed by me.

I have been well taught by my life education because of all the hard knocks, and I feel so empowered by my time in this body. I believe that by staying true to myself and persevering through all that could have taken me out of the game, life has given me some low-level superpowers. The ability to know how to depend on myself, to be my own pillar of support, almost makes me feel like

I need an action figure, one that could also be pinned to a kitchen wall. Mine would not be as iconic as the draped-in-white, spinning-action of the Jesus Action Figure floating above Bethlehem, it could never be. But perhaps mine could be a harbinger of hope, a bald, hoodie-wearing reminder that, with self-reliance and a refusal to give up, even life's deepest hurts sow the seeds for its greatest blessings.

THE MIDDLE

I do not always show up in life in fantastic, exemplary ways. Regardless of how long I have been immersed in wellness, it would be irresponsible of me to act as if I am not as much of a work in progress as anyone else is, someone who has his own stories in which the less-than-ideal patterns of reaction get triggered despite best intentions. I have shown up in life in less than flattering ways, and to recount my stories for commonality to be found without being honest about those moments would be disingenuous. I would be a big, fat liar if I said that I never lose my sense of kindness, calm, or clarity.

A couple of years ago, as I entered the building I live in through the garage, I saw a note pinned to the community bulletin board as I was waiting for the elevator. It was written in childlike handwriting with "HI PEOPLE" written in huge, colourful letters at the top of the page with this written underneath:

"My name is _____ and I am 9 years old I live in this building and I Love dogs I am wondering if I can comeover and play with your dog if yes, can you pleas call my grandpa and tell us what time is good for you. Number: ___ ___ ____."

I saw this note and immediately fell in love with it, charmed to the teeth at the innocence and honesty of this kid who just wanted some time with a dog. I am wholeheartedly a dog person and currently a dog dad, so the note endeared me to the kid even more. However, just when I was feeling that heart squeeze at the sweetness of it all, I began to consider responding to the request and that was when the spiral began.

"So sweet! I wonder which kid this is? I must have crossed paths with her at some point in the building."

"I have a dog! I wonder if she would want to hang out with Willow!?"

"She would most likely come hang out at our place to play with the dog."

"I am not sure I want a kid coming to hang out in our place."

"If we let it happen once, will we start getting knocks on the door at 7:30 in the morning out of the blue because she wants to hang out with the dog again?"

"I am not sure I want to get that ball rolling, having to make room for a kid to hang out in our place, especially if it becomes a habit."

I know this sounds harsh, but I chose to not have children simply because I like my life as it is. I love other people's kids, most of the time. I have never felt the pull to be a parent, apart from parenting my dogs throughout the years and finding myself in the parental role of caring for and accompanying the countless students and people I work with. Whatever need I may have to parent is completely fulfilled, nothing wanting in that department. I also recognize that in many fundamental ways, I am way too involved with my own life and career to even consider prioritizing a child's needs over my own. I recognize that many of you reading this would immediately feel compelled to tell me how it is for that exact reason that I *should* have kids, to experience the spiritual brilliance associated to the selflessness of raising another human being's needs above my own. I have heard it countless times before. And while that might very well be a possibility, trust me when I say that it is the last thing I want, as evidenced by the moment I had in England with one of my godsons when he was very young.

While staying with my friends, I told them that as long as I was over at theirs, they should consider going out for dinner, just the two of them. They had two children under five years of age, and I wanted to let them go and get a taste of the life that existed outside of their roles as parents. They quickly took me up on the offer and left me at theirs with their kids for a few hours over dinner time. I sat in the lounge with the boys watching tv, and at one point the older of the two told me he needed the toilet. I told him to go ahead, quickly wondering why he was letting me know but then letting that thought evaporate as he left the room. About ten minutes later, from the other side of the house where the bathroom was, I heard him yell, "Braaa-aaa-m, I'm finished!" I sat with my other godson, quietly curious as to why I needed to be so informed about that status of his bowel movement, and half-committedly replied, "Ok!". I settled back into the sofa and continued watched TV when, a few minutes later, he yelled again, louder this time, "BRAAA-AAA-M, I'M *FINISHED*!" I looked at his brother and pointed towards the other side of the house with a look on my face that said something to the effect of how strange I found the whole situation, replied a little louder, "Ok!" and then once again got back into the show we were watching. A minute later, at full-rage volume, came the last call, "BRAM! I'M FINISHED!"

I got up off the sofa and walked across the house to the closed bathroom door through which I could see, thanks to the frosted glass pane in the door, my godson still seated on the throne. He could see my figure through the door as well, to which he said accusingly, "I'm finished!", to which I replied, "I know! You have told me three times now!" I will never forget his reply. "No! I'm finished! You need to wipe me!"

If you could have seen, or even just heard, my reply to him, you would have understood just how instinctual and visceral it was. "Noooooooooooooooooooooooooooooooooooooooo", is what came out of my mouth, uttered almost in a zombie-esque groan. "Yes!", he replied. I reluctantly opened the door. He then held out the package of wet wipes, hopped off the toilet seat, turned so that his back was facing me, spread his legs wide apart, and then bent over to make sure that I knew where my responsibilities lay. I was traumatized. I took care of business and decided that when my friends got home, there would be a can of hellfire that I would need to unleash on them. When they did, and I tried, they broke down in such hysterical laughter than any semblance of resentment I may have been harbouring dissipated when I broke down with them.

Bringing it back to the girl from my building, as horrible as it sounded in my brain as the internal dialog bounced around, I did not want to deal with a child. I did not want a kid that I did not know in my space, and I did not want to open the door to having to deal with repeated visits. It sounds cranky and petulant, I know, but that was truly how I felt about it.

My aversion to having children was reinforced decades ago in the most unexpected of ways. Over twenty-five years ago I went to a family dinner at a relative's house shortly after I got my first dog. As everyone was hanging out having drinks and nibbles, one of my relatives pulled me aside and said, "Congratulations on getting your dog! He looks beautiful! I want you to know that if I knew about dogs before I had my kids, I would not have had my kids."

I immediately started laughing, both out of nervous reaction as much as from disbelief, unsure of whether or not I was understanding what I was being told. I soon realized I was the only one laughing, as my relative's face was dead serious. I was then told, "I am serious. If I knew about dogs before I had my kids, I would not have had my kids." And before I knew it, I was standing alone in the room wondering if that had just happened. And then I had the pleasure of going back to mingling with the children who had just been referred to, trying to maintain composure while knowing that a simple trip to the SPCA might have altered their very existence.

Perhaps that little gem of a moment somehow contributed to how I immediately shut down the notion of inviting that girl from my building to hang out with my dog. Perhaps not. However, when I look back on the situation now, I can see how I went from one extreme (feeling sweetness at the girl's note) to another (no way am I getting involved) instead of considering how I might have been able to find some sort of middle ground in which I could have introduced my dog to this girl in a context of my own making. That kind of decision-making, the one that is made from the middle, is what I now strive for as a life practice using mindful attention.

I used to feel a real affinity towards Vishnu, the grand preserving force of the universe according to Hindu mythology. Vishnu is said to keep a watchful eye over Earth, looking out for signs of imbalance within humanity. When trouble seems to reign and humans are lost and confused, it is said that Vishnu will come down to Earth in one of various life forms/incarnations to reset the balance. He is known to be the force that rights wrongs and brings some semblance of harmony, justice, and order back to humanity when we fallible humans lose our way. I innately feel a Vishnu-like sense of vigilance, an awareness of what is going on, mindful of all the life factors and details unfolding around me which add weight to each side of the scales of justice, tolerance, fairness, and equality. When deficiencies or imbalances in these qualities present themselves, the need to reset the balance and right what I see as contributing to wrong can overtake my faculties before awareness of my behaviour is present. And let me be clear, I do not hold myself up to the status of a god, far from it. I, most likely, am still healing the inner child who could not speak his truth. Regardless, this inclination can sometimes be helpful, other times feed the flame of conflict and amplify the very energies I am objecting to, but it often pulls me away from the middle, away from neutral awareness, away from where and how I want to be going forwards.

I recognize that I am sensitive to intolerance, to injustice, to oppression and suffering. I want harmony and peace in life. I want people to get along and I want freedom and equality for everyone.

I want to see kindness and acceptance in the world. And as I get older, I realize that if I really am committed to working and operating from The Middle, what I want to see is what I need to work on within myself, because I can be impatient and intolerant, devoid of kindness and acceptance, while simultaneously growing intolerant to intolerance and antagonistic behaviour from others. This process is the impetus for me to sit down with my own mind, analyze and reflect on how I basically have no right to expect to see any of what I hope for in the world around me until I can own and manage how it all arises within me. I mean, seriously, feeling intolerance arise in the presence of other people's intolerance is making me intolerant to those who are intolerant, making me the intolerant one! I end up contributing to the energy which I object to! I amplify the vibration that disturbed my peace! Physician, heal thyself! And so I try, I do my mindful best, in full awareness that when I get exposed to blatant displays of bad behaviour or meanness, my unchecked default is to lose my sense of decorum and mindful awareness.

The personal growth work I do almost daily is to find the middle as often as possible, a practice that is evocative of the first practice of the Buddhist Noble Eightfold Path, which is *Right View*. When I come back to this middle, I find a perspective that shows me just how quickly and stubbornly I can get caught in one half of a pair of opposites. All sensations, emotions, and thoughts co-arise with their opposites. Duality is the basis of life. You-me, night-day, happy-sad, comfort-pain, this choice-that choice; we are always in a navigating-opposites dance, one which occasionally feels like a tightrope walk. I have jokingly said for years that when I got to old age, I would be that crotchety dude who yells obscenities and has no filter, like that pair of old guys in the Muppets who sit in the balcony and take the piss out of everyone. The truth is that

I would much prefer to not be harboring the energies that hurt me, that land as the felt sense of dis-ease. I would much rather continue to seek out the middle, the place from where I do not need to let unprocessed impulses get the better of me but can observe them from a place of neutral awareness and know that I am doing less harm, to myself and to others.

I got tweaked into mild reaction years ago when a student came up to me after a class I had taught to tell me how incredible it was, and in the same breath, told me that taking the class had cost her an extra sixty dollars because she was so immersed in the class that she had forgotten to pay the parking meter her car was parked at and was now certain that she had a parking ticket waiting for her when she left the studio. I ordinarily would have laughed jokingly at a comment like that one, but she was not laughing. Her face was dead serious, and I quickly clued into the fact that she was, in a passive aggressive way, trying to shift her frustration onto me. Now, as far as I can remember from the class, she didn't get a phone call from a ticketing agent letting her know in real time that she got a ticket, let alone one for such a specific amount like $60. With all this bouncing around in my head, I laughingly replied (most likely with a wee bit of a defensiveness) by saying that I hoped that she wasn't putting the parking ticket on me, as if it were my doing that she had forgotten about the meter. She gave me a cheeky smile and said as she walked away, "It is kind of your fault." And she meant it. My defenses got tweaked by her comment when, in hindsight, I would have loved to have met her from the middle, from a place of laughter, compassion, and complicity. She may have walked into that class as a student, but she ended up being my teacher that day.

Another moment in which my intention backfired magnificently took place as I was driving home one evening after teaching at the yoga studio. I drive a moped around the city when winter is not inflicting its Siberian death hold on us and when I first started driving it around, I found myself a target for the rage that other drivers directed my way as I passed them on the roads. I was not encumbered by the smaller spaces that their cars were unable to fit through and could easily zip by on my little two-wheeler. Throughout the years, I have had drivers, usually male, ragingly yell crazy obscenities at me, and once was even almost driven off the road by a guy in a pickup truck who was so annoyed at my having passed him that he tried to drive his truck into me. Luckily for me, my reflexes were quick, and I drove out of the way up onto the sidewalk. Luckily for both of us, I couldn't catch up to him after the so-called assault, because trust me when I say that when the danger of what this guy had just done registered in my brain and nervous system, all I wanted to do was to catch up to him and run *him* off the road. In real moments of oppression or abuse, there is no wellness teacher or thought leader present in my mind. Sometimes something animalistic takes over, sometimes I get so stuck in one half of a pair of opposites that I forget there is any middle to speak of, so I know I have more work to do to not rise to the bait, trust me, but regardless, sometimes there is rage.

One evening after leaving the studio I was teaching at, I was driving home on the scooter and stopped at a red light. I heard some honking behind me, which I attributed as coming from a driver who was taking issue with me. I ignored it. The lesson I had learned when faced with irate drivers was to not engage, to simply ignore and keep going. The honking continued, and as the light turned green and I started to accelerate, the honking grew even more frequent and insistent. And so, I responded in a way that still makes me laugh, and I hope makes you giggle. I kept one hand on the accelerator, and raised the other hand, extended my middle finger, and flipped the bird to whoever was honking like that behind me. The honking stopped. I kept driving and gradually got home, parked, and checked my phone to find a text from the studio manager who is also a friend, telling me that she had seen me driving and had tried to get my attention to say hi, but was rewarded by getting the finger. Not my proudest moment, even if it still makes me laugh.

Responding to life from the middle, for me, is about letting go of emotional impulse, and it is because of one experience in particular that I am even more mindful of doing that. The cringiest of cringe-worthy moments that stands out in my memory occurred when I was headed downtown to meet someone. I had some trouble finding a parking space for the moped, eventually finding one at the very front of the curb a few blocks away from where I was meeting my friend. I parked perpendicularly to the car parked next to me, put my helmet in the storage area beneath the seat and locked the moped. Suddenly I heard the car's ignition roar to life, and the person in the driver's seat (I had not noticed anyone sitting there) advanced the car until the bumper was two inches away from my bike and then stopped but kept the motor running. I looked through the front windshield and saw a woman in her late sixties or seventies staring back at me, so I approached the passenger side of the car with a puzzled look on my face and asked her,

"Why did you do that? I'm parked legally and was nowhere near your car before you drove it up to me."

Her reply, *"En français, s'il vous plaît!"* (In French, please!)

My reply, *"Je suis stationné correctement, pourquoi avez-vous avancé votre véhicule?"* (I am properly parked, why did you advance your vehicle?).

She shrugged, looking at me with a grin that told me she just wanted to antagonize me. As a reply, I took out my phone and took some pictures of her car parked two inches away from my bike, and then I went to the back of her car to photograph her license plate. She began yelling that I was not permitted to photograph her license plate. I told her (in English) that it was completely within my rights considering I believed she intended to cause harm to my property, to which she yelled at me to speak French. And then I lost it. In not my proudest moment, I told her in good old Québécois, *"Vous voulez que je vous communique en français? Très bien, va chier."* (You want me to speak to you in French? Ok, go fuck yourself.)

The unjustified rudeness, the seeming injustice of her antagonistic behaviour, awakened some sort of animalistic response in me that used to emerge at the first indication of meanness or cruelty but which I had been working on to curb. I intentionally did not want to lose my temper on anyone, especially a woman in her sixties or seventies, but her blatant antagonism pulled me right out of the middle. The part of me that has such a low tolerance for inexplicable and unsolicited bad behaviour took over, and I became stuck in fury, in rage, in rebellion against the seeming injustice of it all, and remember, this was just a woman stirring shit up with me.

What I have learned is that when this happens, when I lose the middle ground, I not only am reacting to the activating incident or person, I am reacting to all of it, the world of unfairness and injustice, the world of intolerance that makes me so sad, that makes me so mad, to every moment of perceived oppression and abuse that has ever arisen within my awareness. And when that animal instinct kicks in, I go straight for the jugular, even after mindfully trying to stay calm and methodical. I believe boundaries need to be set, absolutely, but they should be healthy boundaries. They should be boundaries in which compassion and wise awareness are present and accounted for, not rigid boundaries in which I show up as some sort of maniac dictator ready to slash an old-age pensioner's tires because she feels like being rambunctious. The incident taught me that there needs to be a middle ground between verbally assaulting an albeit antagonistic senior and allowing said senior to be abusive and oppressive. I am still learning where the middle is in moments in which emotional reaction would have me act or speak in unhelpful ways. I am definitely doing the work to get there.

Getting pulled away from the middle has also happened in the most hysterical of situations, like the times I was mistaken for a sex worker. The first incident occurred when I was hired to give a yoga class to a group of women as part of a bridal shower. It was a sunny, summer day and I arrived at the address I had been given by the bride-to-be, who opened the door to me and welcomed me into her home. Waiting for me were her female friends and family members, all of whom turned their heads towards me as I entered the room, and as God is my witness, I heard a sharp intake of breath followed by what felt like an eternity of silence. As the collective exhale slowly began, someone asked in what can only be described as a demonic voice, "Is that the stripper?" Needless to say, I kept my clothes on and responded with a very long, drawn out, "Nooooooooooooooooooooo." This actually happened to me again at another bridal shower I was hired for, but the response from the bride quickly dispelled any illusions as to the purpose of me being there. Both moments occurred out of nowhere, so unpredictably, that I felt myself tense up before recognizing the humour in the incidents and finding my way back to the middle.

There was also the morning when I woke up well before sunrise to go teach a yoga class for a company having its global town hall meeting. I was in a cab on my way to the hotel their conference was taking place at, talking to the driver, telling him I was heading to work at this ungodly hour. He asked me what time I was done, to which I replied, "7am". I was incredibly confused when he started laughing, and he kept laughing until he was crying from laughter. I uncertainly chuckled along with him to play the game until he pulled up to the hotel. I paid the fare and upon exiting the vehicle, turned to thank him to see him smiling at me knowingly and winking, as if he was in on some inside joke. In a flash I understood that he thought I was a sex worker and before I could stop it from coming out of my big mouth, I told him, "I teach yoga and meditation. Not orgasms." As someone who does not drink coffee, it was definitely the kickstart I needed to my early day.

On the Greek island of Paros there is a point on the top of the highest hill where all the telecommunication towers are found, right next to the sweetest little church. The small square in front of the church looks out on an almost three-hundred-and-sixty-degree view of the island, the sea around it, and neighbouring islands. Whenever I think of the perspective I want in moments where I am getting stuck in intolerance or judgement, I bring to mind that view, that center point from which almost all is observable, and I immediately feel my mind, my body's musculature, and my emotional state relax. I find my way back to the middle, but let there be no doubt about it, it is a practice.

Navigating life from the middle can be challenging, especially when working to set boundaries and express myself honestly and authentically. I have learned that I have every right to voice my opinion, even when it may not be popular or provoke confrontation, and I have found myself growing more and more outspoken about the rights and freedoms of those who live on the fringe, those who would be deemed as society's most vulnerable. I have been told throughout the years to not get political in my career, to not be seen choosing a side, as it would hurt me on both a reputational and financial level. As far as I am concerned, no one can do the work of awakening to reality, to all aspects of what is, whether it be through spiritual methods or not, without emerging with an opinion. You cannot be awake in this world without becoming aware of the bullshit, hypocrisy, inequality, and overall unfairness that seem to have become normalized over time. But what I have grown to understand in my practice to come back to the middle is that one can set a boundary and have an opinion without getting worked up into a frenzy. I can be awake while also being aware, practicing wisdom, compassion, spiritual sight, and patience as I am witness to injustice, antagonism, bad behaviour, and intolerance. If my intention is truly to not contribute to the energies I object to, then I need to find the middle where I can sit with objection, experience it without it needing to instigate any action at all, and find comfort in the discomfort. Get the broader view, Paros-style.

I believe that finding the middle is actually coming back to the start. Most of us begin life as little baby creatures who exist in the middle, not getting caught up in any one opposite for too long as long as we are cared for and looked after properly. Coming back to the middle is the process of unconditioning from how we are taught to participate in a world where judgement and opinion run rampant and unchecked. If I want to live in a world where intolerance and inequality diminish, then I need to do my own work in checking myself when I am getting stuck in one half of a pair of opposites and find my way back to the middle, back to the start, before I was taught to unleash my unprocessed emotions and judgements onto others, even in the name of righting perceived wrongs. I would like to think that this type of example could inspire others to do the same, that we can all come back to a starting point and begin again. I believe that this is how healing happens, how we find calm in the chaos, how we find that perspective of wise awareness from where we have an almost three hundred- and sixty-degree view and can appreciate and find value in all that is, especially that which awakens our objection.

THE WAY THE LIGHT FALLS

Why is it that we human beings are our own worst enemies? What is it about the workings of the mind and our biology that find us falling into the *Lord of the Flies* narrative so quickly, so often, and so predictably? What is it about how we operate in the world that allows history to repeat itself, that facilitates hurting and traumatizing and damaging each other? Why are we so unable to live and let live instead of allowing judgement and oppression to reign?

We need love. We need compassion. Collectively and individually, on all levels of how we live our daily existences, we need more love and compassion. We need them to infiltrate the commonly accepted ways that we engage with each other, at work, at home, with friends, when interacting with perfect strangers. We need them to permeate the policies and structures which our societies have observed and adhered to for centuries, archaic structures that were established in different times when decisions were born from necessity and love was a luxury available to the fortunate few. Generations before us would have scoffed at the content of this book. They would have, within the blink of an eye, dismissed any talk of emotions or healing, simply because the times they were living in were defined by the need to survive scarcity, wartime, pandemics, poverty, and generalized instability. The "get-on-with-it" mentality was the only option when trying to simply keep the stomach full and the body sheltered. If one could find a job, one held onto that job for dear life, regardless of whether the job was ideal. If one could find a spouse to marry, one held onto that spouse for dear life, regardless of whether it was a love match. Decisions were born out of necessity, and there was no time or space for discussing the cognitive, emotional, or physical fallout of trying to survive. One just got on with it.

Today, even as people around the world are experiencing some or all of those survivalist conditions and situations, the dialog in the zeitgeist is very much directed towards healing and discussing what previously was considered inappropriate. Instead of adhering to the best practices of decades past which promoted obedience and productivity over well-being, outdated operating structures and systems are being dismantled and new ways to include individual wellness and identity are being prioritized. And that is an indication that we were due, even overdue, for more kindness, gentleness, understanding, compassion, and love. We need more of all of it. On the daily. And as I know that none of us have the right to expect anything from the experience of life that we ourselves are not putting into practice and contributing to, I want to share with you a tool that I have used for decades. This tool has proven to be monumentally helpful in ensuring that I come back to a compassionate perspective when initial response presents as anything but. Let me tell you about The Way the Light Falls.

Because of my experiences, I have grown to understand how fear and suffering recognize themselves in other people, in other beings, regardless of how or where they manifest. As a child moving into adolescence who managed suffering, I was able to quickly suss out my fellow soldiers in the battle of happy versus sad, which often bonded me to others as I found commonality. What was an even more surprising by-product of knowing suffering intimately was that when exposed to erratic or extreme behaviour in others, I innately understood that their behaviour was the product of *their* suffering. I understood that their wounds were motivating the way they were showing up in that moment. Although I did not have the vocabulary or maturity to intellectually piece all of that together, I nonetheless was eventually able to tap into a deeper knowing, a compassion, for how unhappiness and misfortune were at the root of other people's erratic behaviour. Understanding how the fear and suffering which stem from trauma affected me intuitively taught me to manage my own uneasiness and empathize with others instead of responding by othering or bolting away from what was making me feel uncomfortable. And for some unknown reason, when I would see or think about these people with that innate x-ray of compassion, it was as if a filter would descend over them. It was about the way the light fell over how I saw them and their situations. I never knew why, I never even questioned it, but it was like an old, soft-glow-tinged 1970's sheer curtain with nubby threads imposed itself on my thinking and perception. If you have ever seen a film or series in which someone is reminiscing and their memories are being played out tinged with sunlight coming from an upper corner of the shot, dousing the entire scene in a soft energy of sunlight and wistfulness, then you know what I am referring to. The way the light falls in the moments I am presented with other people's suffering marks them for me and has done since I was a child.

As I grew older and began to study yoga, mindfulness, and Hinduism, and as I became more aware of the differences between corporeal and energetic identification, I began to understand that the filter I had grown accustomed to had a purpose. It helped me filter out the energetic noise so that I could see past the traumas, the insecurities, the battles, the adversity, and the suffering to reveal the fallible human at the core of all of it. The ability I had to see past the facades of bulletproof-ness and armouring became an innate mindful, daily practice for me. The practice has grown from recognizing when the filter was imposing itself to imposing it mindfully and intentionally. When faced with someone acting oppressively, violently, erratically, or unhappily, I now cognitively pull out The Way The Light Falls so I can interrupt the initial reaction they may be triggering in me. Of course, the occasional flareup of emotional reaction still arises in the presence of volatile energy, but I have gotten much better at flexing the muscle of recognition repeatedly until I find myself able to respond clearly and compassionately to someone's extreme mood or comportment. This is me intentionally operating from Self energy instead of a cognitive part that has been tweaked into emotional reaction. This is me growing. This is me doing better and doing it on purpose. Having this mindful tool has been the x-factor allowing me to diffuse situations instead of fuel them, finding stability and calm instead of division and resentment.

The Way the Light Falls is the tool that I continue to foster to stay closer to the vibration of accompaniment in times when its opposite could easily integrate itself. The mindlessness with which people allow their wounds and traumas to self-perpetuate is, as far as I am concerned, at the root of most, if not all, injustice, violence, and oppression. The ways in which we hurt each other as human beings are exactly the ways in which we are contributing to our own demise, largely because through the lenses of ego and rigidity, we find ways to justify how and why we hurt others. We allow fear, shame and grief to fuel the patterns of rejection, abandonment, dismissal, neglect, division, and othering and because they are familiar to us, we rarely consider that perhaps this "being human" thing is actually a massive test. We rarely consider whether, with every moment we find those energies dominating, we are being presented with the opportunity to do the unthinkable, which is to stop them dead in their tracks. Perhaps with every traumatic event, we are offered, in real time, the opportunity to finally break the cycles of trauma and violence by doing something differently, by refusing to allow these energies which have haunted humanity for eons to continue doing their damage unchecked and untethered. Perhaps this life thing is just a global classroom asking us to learn from experience, to recognize when we have veered away from the curriculum and to gauge our own peace and degree of calm as an indicator of whether we are sticking to the syllabus responsibly or not.

Not being tricked into the mindlessness required to allow anger, fear, rage, hatred, violence, oppression and othering to continue their unchecked paths of destruction requires me to intentionally and mindfully apply the filter of The Way the Light Falls, to see past the chaos and what so easily makes discomfort arise. It is not always easy, and there moments in which I absolutely fail. But I bounce back, knowing that I need to apply a mindful lens that enables me to see through the symptoms of trauma so that the humanity can be made visible. The Way the Light Falls has always been, for me, what strips away the layers of division and defense, only to reveal the flame of the unifying force that we all are born of and ache to return to throughout the often-tumultuous journey of life.

You know the way that you can hold space, time, and love for the people in your life you treasure the most? The way you can put aside everything you are doing, even for a little while, to be available and compassionate for your friends and family members when they feel the heaviness of a life that is, in its essence, volatile, unpredictable and, often, unfair? If so, then you know something about The Way the Light Falls. You know that it can be more of a mindset than a literal filter, you know that it speaks to a form of selfless giving, compassionate understanding, and loving kindness, a mindfulness practice which is incorporated in real time during real events and situations. You have the ability to draw on your own version of The Way The Light Falls to see through the presenting vibrations of chaos and discomfort and do something that returns you closer to the vibration of love. As a dear friend of mine has alluded to countless times throughout the years, we may not know the full benefits of living as close to the vibration of love as we could do, but we certainly know what the opposite is like. Humanity today, as I write these words, has never seemed more divided or fragmented, or, at least, that is the narrative we are being fed by media and government. That division and fragmentation is the result of not doing our own healing, and of not allowing others to do theirs.

We know what division looks and feels like. We know the insidious nature and devastation of hatred. We know how the easy game of judging based on labels and appearances fragments us from each other and tricks us into believing that we are alone, not in any way connected to each other or part of a greater whole. Yes, the ways in which we are different one from the other matter in the game of life and dictate the degrees of privilege and resistance we will be afforded and subjected to. And yes, those differences, what makes each of us unique, should actually be celebrated instead of used as ammunition to other and discriminate. But what lies underneath all that the mindless among us use as justification to perpetuate their trauma and hurt is actually what unifies us. We have all landed in these bodies, separate and unique, through the accidents of birth we are subjected to and we spend the rest of our lives believing the labels that are affixed to the appearances of those bodies. We allow ourselves to exist in this first-degree existence where who we are is identifiable by how we look instead of how we are. We are not these bodies. We are the energy, every single one of us, which animates these bodies into being. If we recognized each other as an energy animating a body in the same way that a body animates a moving vehicle, we would ease off on judging the body. Because that is what human beings do. They judge each other's body thinking that they are judging the person, the being inside the body, but they are not. They are simply judging the vessel, not the essence of it. This practice of looking beyond the obvious, of recognizing the evident even if it is not identifiable using the five senses, is how we heal, both individually and collectively. It is what we need to prioritize and elevate in order to heal and establish a sustainable path forward. And so, if we know what living life further away from love results in, then why would we not apply whatever version of The Way the Light Falls we can tap into to bring us closer to more love, more of the time?

The biggest challenge for me, and I suspect, for you as well? To mindfully observe The Way the Light Falls in my own moments of shifting mood/emotion/thought/sensation. To apply that understanding, love, and compassion to myself when there are moments of concealment, when all the higher learning and higher-Self tools vanish as if they had never existed. To treat myself the same way I would treat another whose suffering had gotten the better of them. I believe that we have an often-endless capacity to offer others what we most ravenously need for ourselves, and I believe that, on some levels, we have been taught that to be kind to ourselves is a form of selfishness that is somehow unacceptable. I wholeheartedly disagree. Know that no one can do for you what only you can, no one can know the contents of your mind and heart better than you, no one can respond in real time when what you so desperately need makes itself apparent. We all need to know that we can flex that muscle of compassion and understanding for ourselves. We need to understand that we deserve all of it and more, we always have.

Recognise that your stories, your experience, all of it weaves together to form the narrative of you, the tale that accompanies your you-ness, and that narrative is valuable and deserves being honoured and nurtured. Find compassion and love for yourself using a practice that allows you to see yourself, your suffering, and your own life experience through The Way the Light Falls. And then try it with others. Humanity becomes its own worst enemy when the cycles of harm, trauma and fear are left unchecked. Applying The Way The Light Falls is a graceful mindfulness tool that caringly interrupts those cycles, a way to respond differently when reaction abounds. And differently is how we must operate going forward. If we want to see a different outcome of peace and unity, we must respond instead of reacting, with the clear intention of finally doing something differently. This is healing.

CONCLUSION

I have heard it said that every generation must know its own suffering. What I have learned is that every person must know their own suffering. And while the culture that I grew up in offered no preparation for or salves to soothe the suffering that was in store for me, what I have learned through my awareness of all suffering is that with a mind left to its own devices, suffering is inevitable.

I do not believe that we are meted out our fair (or seemingly unfair) doses of it just to see how many times we can get knocked down and get back up again. I do not believe in the concept of life as a game in which it is just a matter of time before everyone stays down after the final blow is dealt. I believe that all the situations (and their resulting consequences) which fall under the umbrella of suffering are meant to be seen as part of life's curriculum, the education we were enrolled in at birth. They are meant to be known as opportunities for growth. They are meant to be recognized as life lessons through which we become clearer, more evolved versions of ourselves. They are meant to be recontextualized as opportunities to finally turn toward hardship and that which threatens emotional overwhelm and do the deep cognitive and spiritual work of healing without fear. For those of us who strive to improve the experience of life for ourselves and for others, it is essential to recontextualize and examine our suffering, to do so for *all* suffering, to welcome and sit with it, to examine all aspects of how it lands in the body and the mind. This is life's classroom.

Much of my suffering has been related to having to find my place and establish my identity in relation to an unforgiving economic, cultural, socio-political landscape and world in which individuality is only rewarded when it pleases the masses. Feeling alone, isolated and different in formative years, not fitting into commonly accepted and celebrated archetypes, has absolutely contributed to the suffering I have known. I also know that that experience has served as the platform from which I could begin to pursue whatever balms I could find in Eastern philosophies and practices, as well as in psychotherapeutic modalities, to understand how to engage with and transcend my suffering. To know my own suffering and how to approach it is to know everyone's suffering and have a template to accompany them. Of this I am sure because I found those balms and they worked, as does the accompaniment which informs the work that I do with others. Through the transcendence and recontextualization of my struggles, I found what was worth sharing, while also amassing some great stories.

In seeking and navigating the avenues and byways in search of healing, I discovered the most fundamental of truths related to suffering staring me right in the face: our culture does not set us up to thrive. Our culture is predicated on the normalization of struggle and suffering. Healing and prioritizing health is costly, on many levels, largely because we are not taught through conventional avenues of education how to navigate cognitive/emotional/physical obstacles and challenges. From early on in life we are put into educational systems which teach us how to read, write, study subjects and then eventually choose one of those subjects to focus on so we can eventually do it to earn money in the workplace. This is how succeeding at the game of life is presented to us: get an education, make money, pay taxes, make more money, buy more things, pay more taxes on those things, play the game. With more money comes more consumption, with more consumption come more taxes to pay, the endless pursuit continues, keep playing the game. Playing the game demands that we devote our time and energy to the pursuit of trying to keep our heads above water and not get carried out into the sea of financial debt, social rejection and general failure when we find ourselves incapable of thriving in a system that has no interest in our individuality, wellness or well-being. We are gaslit into believing that these avenues of existence will set us up to succeed when the opposite is, actually, the case. Success was never about money or material abundance, not solely, yet that has been the dangling carrot we have been taught to chase at the expense of all else. We are groomed to participate in and contribute to an economic system in which health, wellness, individuality and "you-ness" is pretty much irrelevant. I believe it is fair to say that we are thrust into a system that sets us up to fail, and if we believe that that is all there is, that trying to win at the game of life is everything, then there will be suffering.

We are not taught through conventional avenues of education how to take care of the body, how to take care of the mind, how to process extreme emotions, thoughts, and physical sensations, or how to value and appreciate ourselves as separate and whole from money and the economic system. We are not taught what to do when we look in the mirror and feel shitty about what we see. We are not taught what to do when we get broken up with. We are not taught what to do when money is tight and the bills are already overdue. We are not taught what to do when we lose a job. We are not set up to succeed in any other aspect of life aside from that which speaks to the economic system we are trained to participate in. We are not set up to thrive. We are, however, set up to struggle. The absence of preparation required to "human", combined with feeling alien and community-less in my life, amplified my struggle, exacerbated the suffering I was meted out in childhood and adolescence. Yet instead of staying little and afraid, something inside of me knew to push back against the injustice and inequity I was myself oppressed by. Something I never questioned knew to rebel, to disobey, to follow an unknown and unpaved path through which I would find something of value.

In the game of life, individuality and otherness is not celebrated, conformity and obedience is. To be yourself in the world honestly and unapologetically can be one of the most courageous things you can do. It can also be the most dangerous. And yet, as far as I am concerned, to know and express yourself into the world is the purpose of life and the only healthy, sustainable path worth following. It can also be the murkiest one, being that person who dares to disobey, who dares to do things differently, who dares to question, to rebel, to defy. I believe this is the path of truth. It is also the path of suffering.

To remain steadfast in the mission to know and express yourself honestly and authentically gradually becomes a spiritual practice of knowing the difference between yourself and your Self. To identify who and how you are as a person is the lower case "s" self. To identify who and how you are as an energy that animates the body-container taps into the upper-case "S" Self. The latter requires knowing that the consciousness which animates the container we know to be the body is universal consciousness, the energy of life that expresses itself through, and as, all that exists. It is the energy which directed me to rebel, to disobey, to find my own way into my life and the world instead of continuing to fall prey to the fear which informed by childhood. To know and express one's Self requires knowing that the consciousness that expresses itself through these human bodies also can learn to identify itself using the faculties of the human brain, allowing universal consciousness to, as Carl Sagan so perfectly put it, "know itself". To know and express one's Self also requires being able to contextualize one's experience of life and the suffering that that it has been shaped and defined by. To then be able to relay the stories and the narratives of that experience from Self is to finally transcend the first-degree experience, to move from "self" to "Self". Transcending the first-degree experience enables us to be able to witness and observe what has been through a different lens, thereby training us to do the same with what is yet to come on this journey of life. We develop spiritual sight and understanding, finding connection where previously disconnect lay. We become privy to the bigger picture, allowing us to let go of the daily dramas and play the long game, not getting tweaked into emotional reaction by every little thing which arises in the changing landscape. And when we do get tweaked, despite our best efforts and understanding? We know how to process what has arisen so that it falls away quicker, not propelling us into erratic behaviour or mindless rumination. We become cognizant of what suffering really is: resistance to the lessons that life has in store for all of us. This knowing gives us the opportunity to stop resisting, to lean into what lands uncomfortably, to look for what can be gleaned from the situation and ask how the lessons might perhaps exist to empower us going forward. To transcend the narrative, to transcend the suffering, to find comfort in the uncomfortable, to find stability in the unstable, to find an unchanging perspective in a world defined by change is, quite simply, why we are here. It is what we are meant to do with the time we have in these bodies, and once we have captured a glimpse of this new way of seeing and being, we find freedom. We find calm. We find peace. We find fulfillment. We find that thing that we believed would be waiting for us if we followed all of the commonly accepted protocols that the game of life had been marketed to us as containing, but which we were left craving for when none of that amounted to more than simply playing a game.

Moving from self to Self is about transcending fear and how it keeps us in a perpetual state of mindlessness. Mindlessness is the foundation of allowing fear and scarcity to lead. Mindlessness is being without awareness and without tactics to meet and witness the menacing thoughts, the intense emotions, and/or the physical sensations which present when we live in self, allowing them to control us and thereby control our contentment and overall sense of safety and stability. From a storytelling or mythological perspective, and to reference Joseph Campbell's *The Hero's Journey*, every one of us is on a path which will occasionally be littered with obstacles or threats, much like Frodo in *The Lord of the Rings*. We are all Frodo on our own search for the ring/sword/grail, and in the moments in which our minds could easily convince us to give in, give up or be led astray, it is the mindfulness practices we apply that will keep us in wise response and forward momentum. In every instance when negativity erupts in this human mind and body we each inhabit, we are being asked to strip it of the hold

Leading from Self means recognizing our own innate validity and power while neutrally observing and releasing the fear-based tendrils of the past which would restrict forward momentum. Life is uncertain and always will be. The sooner we awaken to the understanding that being ashamed, insecure, or afraid accomplishes very little, the faster we will be able to tune into Self, into our own innate power, abilities, and potential. This is how we will move towards the future versions of ourselves and of the stories that are waiting for us. And we will do it fearlessly. We can either tiptoe our way through life afraid of the landmines of tragedy that each of us will inevitably, at one time or another, step on, or we can move forward fearlessly, expecting the occasional landmine, steeped in the mindful intention to continue that forward momentum without getting interrupted when something detonates. At the end of it all, it all becomes a story, and keeping that in mind helps contextualize the moments that might previously have left us disempowered and interrupted.

By understanding this journey of narrative guiding us closer and closer to Self, we finally recognize our value and worth. We know our individual power. We hold ourselves in the highest esteem when we previously only held others to those heights, understanding that by the simple fact of being, we are miraculous. Knowing ourselves to be on equal footing as every other person on the planet levels the playing field, awakening us to not only know, but truly LIVE the understanding that we are as miraculous, as strong, as able, and as great as we choose to believe we are. And that power, that knowing of thy Self, is what we are not taught to tap into as we are groomed for the game of life, but you know what? It is the missing, magic ingredient that introduces thriving into the game of life. Celebrating and owning what makes you *you* as you play the game of life a) changes the rules so that you are not playing according to the archaic ones that everyone else has unconsciously accepted as valid, b) helps direct you towards thriving by accessing deeper understanding of this experience of self vs Self, and c) inspires others to perhaps break out of the confines of their adopted beliefs so that thriving can become a communal experience, not relegated to the courageous few. The miracle and value exist in the understanding that we ARE, that we, as these energies that inhabit these bodies, are the manifestation of the mystery of life. Consciousness embodying a human body, expressing itself into the world uniquely, an expression that is unique in all of time, one that the world would not have if fear and insecurity were left unchecked. Mindlessness kills recognition of the miracle. This life in a body is a miracle. YOU are a miracle, as am I, as we all are.

The biggest realization of all, the one that changes everything, lands immediately once we can clearly and viscerally understand that "I am not the thinker or the doer" in the experience of living. To know one's Self as an energy that observes and expresses itself through the thinker/doer is to understand the spiritual teaching that we are not our bodies. Eckhart Tolle so succinctly referred to this concept of reidentification in his book *The Power of Now* when recounting how he could no longer stand to live with himself, thereby realizing that if he could no longer live with himself, there must be two of him, the "I" and the "self" he could no longer tolerate. Epiphanies like his are available to every one of us, guiding us to the knowledge that we are the energy that animates and uses the body it to express itself into the world through an expression that is unique, one of a kind in all of time. In those moments of spiritual grace and pure presence, we, with spiritual sight and understanding, can observe not only the thinker/doer doing its thing, but also the tendency, the learned, patterned behaviour, to slip into identification with the thinker/doer as easily as the body inhales and exhales with no instruction or direction needed. And with that identification comes identification with everything the thinker/doer has ever thought, done, or said, which, in my case, is the Bram story. And with that identification comes the ego's need to stick to that narrative, to stick to those stories, to stick to the timelines and decisions and successes and failures. To continue to refer back to them. To continue to speak and write about them, often using the exact same languaging as if reciting from a script. To allow the back story to somehow influence or direct the forth story, the story of what can, might, will be.

What we are left with are stories. Stories to be shared which guide us to a bigger picture understanding of this experiencing of navigating life in a human body and how there may just be more to it than we have been taught to believe. The last story I will tell here beautifully summarizes this.

When I was fourteen years old, I read an article in *Rolling Stone* about a relatively new singer-songwriter whose voice was transfixing those who heard it and whose debut album was getting a lot of attention. Her name was Sinéad O'Connor. I devoured the article, immediately sensing a complicity with her. In hindsight, I can see how suffering recognized itself as I was instantly drawn to her. I went out and bought her album and fell under her spell, listening to her melodic howling and recognizing my own hurt and rage in her protest singing.

As I got older, my love for Sinéad grew. I saw her struggles, cheered her on through her battles with mental illness, lamented and grieved for her when her son committed suicide, and rejoiced when she reappeared on Twitter in the summer of 2023.

I commented on the video she had posted of herself, letting her know how wonderful it was to see her and how many of us loved her, and she acknowledged my message by liking the comment. I was elated. My childhood idol who I felt had grown up with me had acknowledged my existence. I was chuffed.

About two weeks later, I was at home cooking and burned my forearm on the side of a hot pan. When I looked at where the burn was, I noticed it was right over a tattoo I had had done a couple of years earlier, a tattoo of Sinéad's words from her autobiography. "Music is for the things that cannot be discussed" is what I had permanently etched on my body, her words which perfectly evoked the gratitude I felt for her and her music and how they had touched me all those years earlier when life seemed bleak for me. I was gutted that the burn was over her words, and I feared it would permanently scar.

I found out the following day that Sinéad had passed away sometime around when I had burned my arm, and I broke down when I got the news. Actually, before I broke down, I observed myself barking, "No, no, no, no, no, no" uncontrollably as I scoured the internet, hoping I would find nothing confirming the news. When I did indeed find the confirmation I was dreading, I then started crying, weeping for an hour. I cried for this sensitive, beautiful soul who had been so hurt by life, by humanity. I cried for the young version of myself who fell in love with Sinéad and who no longer felt alone in his pain and protest. I cried for the fragility of life and for one more marker of the passing of time. And when I could finally breathe and begin to calm down, I realized the significance of the burn from the day before and went from fearing a scar to hoping for one. I took that burn to be some sort of sign or message from one sensitive soul who knew suffering to another, and I wanted that sign with me for as long possible.

When I had recovered from the shock of her passing, I texted a friend of mine and told her about the burn. Without a moment's hesitation, she asked me, "If the burn could be her trying to let you know something, what would you say her message is?" I did not have to think twice about the answer. I replied, "That there is a degree of connection to which we are completely oblivious. A connection of which we are aware of and part of before we get delivered into a body, and a connection to which we return when we leave the body. There is connection on a level which we are completely unaware." And I believe that, now more than ever. When life gets intense, when hope seems impossible, when division and injustice seem to reign, I remind myself that there is a degree of connection running through everything and everyone on a level to which we are completely unaware. And everything falls back into making some sort of sense. All the stories, all the suffering, all the successes, all the struggles become less important, waning in significance as the burn on my arm throbs ever so slightly and I am reminded of the undercurrent of meaning that roars around and through us as Self, everywhere and all at once.

I have witnessed twists of fate in my narrative which I have quickly identified as fantastic plotlines to the Book of Bram. The suffering throughout these narratives has often seemed unbearable, and yet, despite often believing I was incapable of surviving, I am still here. And if those survival moments, narratives, and plot twists, as well as these pages, have served to show that I am indeed the hero of my own life, then let them also be the homeground from which the entire purpose to my life can be found, which, simply put, is to transcend them all and accompany others, to be a Keeper, to walk alongside those desiring accompaniment on their life journey, to stand in my purpose. My suffering has been, and continues to be, my teacher. The same goes for my successes, for the hard-earned wisdom I have been privy to through persistence and not settling for herd mentality or what others felt was appropriate for me. My stories have been, and continue to be, what I use to connect to others so that all the bickering and finger-pointing and name-calling and othering can be wiped out in one clean swoop of the sword of intention and division can give way to accompaniment, to togetherness, to grace, to connection. What makes the Bram-ness the Bram-ness is simply that which permits others to identify and celebrate their own-ness. As within, so without. We are all of the same -ness, or "Is-ness" as referred to by Jean Klein. Know your -ness to be just that, the platform from which you are meant to connect to and accompany others. This is not just my story. It is yours as well. We are all born of the same energy, like waves coming from the same body of water, and to that body of water we shall return. How and if we recognize ourselves in each other between birth and death of the body is up to us. That is where our work lies. To see beyond the stories and see the soul, recognize the consciousness, understand the journey, know the roaring undercurrent of connection. Thank you Sinéad.

We are all Storytellers. We all have stories, and my stories will trigger contemplation in you, the reader, while yours will do the same for those to whom they are recounted. Tell your stories. We are hungry for them and the accompaniment they will bring. But understand this: you are not your stories. You are the energy that animates and observes the experiences of the protagonist of those stories. That understanding alone will change how you see yourself, how you see life, how you see the time you have to direct the protagonist. Change the story of you that you have been telling yourself all this time. It is time to awaken. Awaken to your truth as the subject of your own experience, an experience that is unique in the details and plot twists while also being communal in this shared experience of consciousness. Awaken to this current of connection which is at the root of all that is, including you and I.

We are not only all Storytellers, but we are also all Keepers as well. We are all in this experience of life, in differing individualities, incarnations and situations, together. And when looking back at our stories, if blessed with that moment at the end of bodily life to ask ourselves, "What was it all for?", let us remember that it may have seemed like it was about the "me", what "I" wanted, needed and felt compelled to do and say, but it was never solely about that. It was always about how the journey to the "me" and the "I" ultimately led us to each other, about how our experiences brought us to, and helped inspire, each other. It was always about how we interact with and affect each other. It was always about not buying into the narrative of individuality and separation and rising above common rhetoric to see how every single one of us has the light and power within to influence and affect others. We are here to be here for, and to take care of, each other, because by doing so, we take care of ourselves. I am because you are. You are because I am. We all are because we all are. We always have been. And we always will be.

Printed in Great Britain
by Amazon